THE CORAL BUILDINGS

OF

SUAKIN

☀ SUAKIN ISLAND ☀

Reconstituted Aerial View as it was in 1900

EL G...

Sh'ainawi Bey's Wakkala

Gordon's Gate

Mohammed Bey Aboud

Mitchell Cotts' Bldg.

Sh. Omar Obeid

Moh Ali Gawish

Gellatéen Hankey's Building

House of Sayda Zeinab el Mirghaniya

Law Courts

Catholic Church

Ferry.

Shennawi Bey's Two Houses

Beit el Basha

National Bank

Mohammed Bey Ahmed

Khorshid eff.

Tea House

Shafa'i Mosque

G.H.Q.

Hanafi Mosque

Beit el Gedid

Post Office

Eastern Telegraph Co.

Merkaz & Customs

Muhafsa

Ferries.

THE CORAL BUILDINGS

of

SUAKIN

by

JEAN-PIERRE GREENLAW

ORIEL PRESS

STOCKSFIELD

LONDON   BOSTON

First published in 1976
by Oriel Press Ltd. (Routledge & Kegan Paul Ltd.)
Branch End, Stocksfield, Northumberland NE43 7NA

Designed at Oriel Studios
Printed and Bound in Great Britain by
Knight & Forster Ltd., Leeds

ISBN 0 85362 158 6

Publication of this book has been generously assisted by
The National Council for Research of the
Democratic Republic of the Sudan

CONTENTS

Preface

		Page
Chapter One	The Town of Suakin	8
Chapter Two	The Story of Suakin	13
Chapter Three	Domestic Life in Suakin	17
Chapter Four	Roshans: Casement Windows	21
Chapter Five	Earlier and Larger Turkish Houses	22
Chapter Six	Smaller Turkish Houses	38
Chapter Seven	Zawias and Mosques	62
Chapter Eight	Egyptian Style Buildings	72
Chapter Nine	Military Buildings	85
Chapter Ten	Building Methods	87
Chapter Eleven	Woodwork	103

PREFACE

THIS BOOK is primarily a collection of architectural drawings of the buildings of the now derelict island-town of Suakin for their aesthetic qualities; it is less concerned with Suakin's history or geographical position. The houses and mosques described were of a remarkable and hitherto unrecorded style and the earlier ones are of uncertain date.

They were an unforgettable sight when they were intact, floating on their flat, oval-shaped island-platform and were admired by all who saw them. It was natural that someone should try to record their architectural qualities while they were still comparatively intact. I am surprised that I was privileged to be that person. I would have expected someone more competent and specialised to have done so before me. But had I not begun, in a casual way, to record them in the 1940's, when the houses were comparatively intact but uninhabited and therefore easy of access, there would have been virtually no houses to record a decade or two later. Today, the visitor to Suakin will find it hard to believe that it ever contained the beautiful houses I have tried to illustrate and describe. He will be equally surprised to learn that they were sufficiently intact, even in 1950, to be recorded with so much detail. Their decay and collapse was unexpectedly rapid, it is true, accelerated to some extent by lack of mutual protection as they fell, but it is natural to ask how and why so unusual an example of a truly remarkable vernacular style of architecture was allowed to disappear so completely and leave its recording to a comparative amateur.

The story of Suakin's sudden decline has been described in detail by a recent writer, D. Roden[1], and I need not, therefore, repeat it here. The principal cause was the building of a new port called Port Sudan at Sheikh Barghout only 40 miles to the north where drinking-water was more plentiful and the harbour better able to cope with modern shipping. This proximity did not allow Suakin to maintain a separate existence yet it was too far away for it to become a suburb. The new port gradually drew away the rich cosmopolitan merchant-population of Suakin who were the occupants and builders of these fine houses, and with no-one to maintain them they soon began to deteriorate and ultimately to disintegrate. The inability of the Sudan Government to preserve these uninhabited houses is understandable.

Buildings without occupants are an anomaly, and though there were numerous appeals and schemes to try to check their disintegration, the proposals could never overcome this basic fact. All came to nothing.

As to the nature of its recording in these drawings, the work lays no claim to scholarship. The material had to be collected when there were no scholars and professionals to do the job. The author's interest was mainly aesthetic and he was not concerned, at the outset, with scrupulous accuracy of detail and measurement. It was only as he was about to leave the country in 1951 that he realized the importance of what he had collected and the unlikelihood of anyone else being able to make use of his unedited material. Most of the drawing-up of buildings had to be done in England from notes, sketches, photographs and maps, and he little realized, at the time, the extent of what he had undertaken. As time went on Suakin quite literally imposed itself on him and has never quite relinquished its hold. Even twenty-five years later he continues to discover unexpected refinements in the style as he draws up individual houses. Such is the power of a work of art (and Suakin was a very considerable work of many sincere and gifted craftsmen), that it can perpetuate the genius of its makers indefinitely. To begin with, he simply made paced-out sketch-plans which he was able to verify and correct in their perimeters, from a large-scale map of the island made by the Sudan Government Survey Department in 1916[2]. The upper floors and window-positions could, in most cases, be checked from photographs, but it was not possible to verify all the dimensions, especially those in the vertical plane. These had to be judged by eye, and here, his training as an artist rather than as a surveyor was of value. It also enabled him to invest the plans and elevations of the houses with a little of the spirit of their builders.

This survey is fairly complete. Some seventy typical buildings, including mosques, out of about three hundred have been fully recorded and sixty of them have been included in this book.

Suakin is an example of a style which can still be seen in Jedda and Massowa, though rapidly disappearing even there. It is the style also of Mecca and Medina and, therefore, of building-methods at the very heart of Islam: methods so dependent on local materials and requirements that they can have changed very little over the centuries — a fact which makes them very difficult to date.

Finally, this is a record of the town, not as it is now, nor even as it was when the author surveyed it, but as it will have looked in its comparatively recent hey-day at the turn of the 20th century.

The initiative of the Sudan Government has resulted in this book and a mission by its author to collect and collate graphic records of the town. He wishes to record his gratitude, especially to the National Council for Research in the Sudan, for making possible the publication of these drawings as a tribute to the genius of Suakin's craftsmen and the sagacity of their patrons.

The personal initiative of Sayed Sammani Yagoub, Secretary of the National Council for Research in the Sudan, and its Director, Sayed Wadiah Habashi, led to the Council's sponsoring of the book on a generous scale. The author wishes to record his appreciation of this fact. He also wishes to acknowledge the help of the many people who enabled him to collect his material: the Sudan Government in the 1940's and the 1950's and University College, Khartoum, for enabling him to visit Suakin often enough to make the record; the late Major E. O. Springfield and Mrs Springfield, and Mr W. T. Clark, then Commissioners of Port Sudan, for their help and hospitality; Mr Trott, the British Ambassador in Jedda in 1951, and Mrs Trott, for enabl-

ing him to study the style in Jedda and to compare the houses in Suakin with inhabited examples there; the late Dr O. G. S. Crawford for the photograph of da Castro's drawing of Suakin; Dr J. Bloss for permission to quote from his articles in Sudan Notes and Records and for aerial photos taken in 1931; Messrs W. W. Wakefield, P. Daniell and others for the loan of photographs, Professor P. L. Shinnie and Mr Neville Chittick, for valuable advice about the text; Professor Miles Danby for recent help and encouragement and to Sayed Bastawi Baghdadi, Head of the School of Fine Art, and Sayed Karamallah, Muhafiz of Port Sudan, and Sayed Gamal el Din el Mubarak for enabling him to visit Suakin again in 1973 and 1974; and to Sayed el Safi in Port Sudan for some interesting last-minute information and corrections.

He also found the remarks of Derek Matthews and Eric Hansen; though made after he had collected his material, useful, coming from experts who, alas, arrived too late to record Suakin in its prime themselves. Matthews did however make a useful summary of the style in the first number of *Kush*[3] in Khartoum in 1954.

Finally, just before going to press, UNESCO enabled him to pay a longer visit to Suakin and, on this occasion, Sayed Nigm el Din Mohammed Sherif, Director of the National Museum, Khartoum, allowed Sayed Mohammed Faig Yusif to accompany him and help him to verify some of the material.

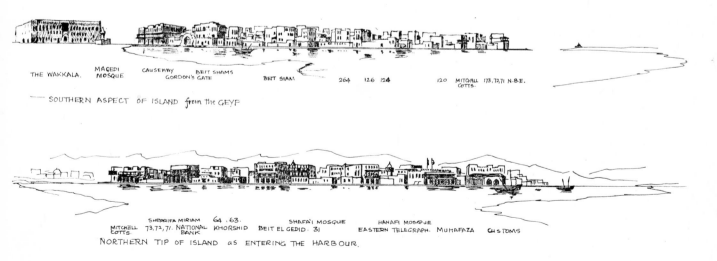

THE WAKKALA.   MAGEDI MOSQUE   CAUSEWAY GORDON'S GATE   BEIT SHAMS   BEIT SIAM   264 126 124   120 MITCHELL 173,72,71 N.B.E. COTTS.

SOUTHERN ASPECT OF ISLAND from the GEYF

SHERRIFA MIRIAM 64 .63.   SHAFA'I MOSQUE   HANAFI MOSQUE
MITCHELL 73,72,71. NATIONAL KHORSHID BEIT EL GEDID. 31   EASTERN TELEGRAPH. MUHAFAZA   CUSTOMS
COTTS.   BANK

NORTHERN TIP OF ISLAND as ENTERING THE HARBOUR.

CHAPTER ONE
THE TOWN OF SUAKIN

"It takes more than putting building-materials together to create architecture, but no one can explain exactly what that more is, except that architecture has a spirit and building has not . . . the structure of a building can be explained and the strength of materials tested, but the spirit of the building, its form and spaces, must be felt in much the same way that the Ancients sensed spirits within the forms of rocks and trees."

A GREAT tradition of architecture, such as that of Islam, can be as clearly discerned in the simpler forms built by ordinary folk in small towns as in the imposing monuments of its great cities. Suakin is an example of a small Turkish town built between the 16th and 20th centuries like other towns situated around the Red Sea coasts; Massawa, Jedda, Hodeida, Assat and Mowka. Some have disappeared; others are in an advanced stage of decay; all are doomed as examples of a vernacular style, and since this book was written Suakin Island-town itself has virtually crumbled away.

There are two kinds of town-building in Arabia and Islamic Africa, each conditioned by different climatic considerations; the inland, desert type, and a type adapted to the requirements of a coastal climate.

The desert style has thick, earth-walls with a characteristic *batter* due to their being thicker at the bottom than at the top, a natural consequence of building homogeneous walls in baked earth without bricks. The rooms are lofty and windowless, except for small openings at the very top allowing sufficient light to get in and the hot air inside the room to escape. The ground-floor quarters are sometimes slightly below ground-level. They provide a cool, cave-like freshness which is welcome in a desert climate and exclude the sun's glare and burning, sand-laden winds. Quite large towns, with such buildings, in some cases impressively walled and fortified, are found in the Moghreb (Morocco), in the Atlas mountains, in the North-African desert oases, Algeria, Lybia, up the Nile to Nubia and the Sudan and in Somalia; in the desert regions of Arabia and on an impressive scale, in Northern Nigeria, Niger, and the Western Sudan. They are built of hand-moulded clods of earth rather than bricks and can be said to be sculpted by hand.

A coastal climate, however, requires a very different kind of building; one which will catch every available sea-breeze and allow it to circulate freely throughout the house, but the hot land-winds and the harsh glare of the midday sun must also be excluded. A style to suit these conditions has been evolved around the coasts of the Red Sea. It consists of two or three-storeyed houses with vertical, not battered, walls pierced by many-shuttered windows and characteristic *mashrabiyas*, large casement-windows projecting out into the street in order to catch the breeze. The internal walls also have ventilating grilles to allow the air to penetrate right into the centre of the house. The staircase acts as an air-well conducting the hot air right out of the house. It is an aerated style, with roof-terraces (*kharjahs*) on which to sleep in the welcome coolness of the

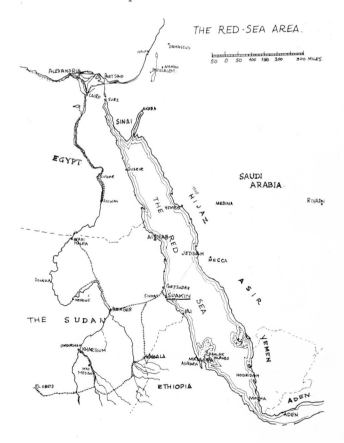

THE RED-SEA AREA.

moon- or star-lit evenings. The little port of Suakin on the Sudan coast of the Red Sea, nearly opposite to Jedda, was an example of this latter style. Its derelict condition and abandoned state permitted this detailed study to be made.

Suakin was a smaller town than Jedda, but its builders were Hedjazis using exactly the same methods and designs as the houses there. The earlier Turkish, as distinct from the later Egyptian houses, were examples of a long-established town-building tradition—tall, white-washed, three and four-storeyed buildings of similar plans and elevations, built in blocks or terraces of three or four at a time, and separated by narrow streets and small clearings. They were adorned with sculpted door-hoods and denticulated parapets and had windows and doors of Java teak which had weathered to a silver-grey. They were possessed of considerable charm, dignity and refinement.

Suakin Island when surveyed had but three or four really large houses, and nearly two hundred smaller ones. It also had two small mosques and at least six *zawias* or private praying-places, and there was a street of small shops. The outside walls of the buildings were white-washed which set off the greyed windows, *mashrabiyas*, and carved wooden doors which were surmounted by their carved stone door-hoods. Its situation on a flat island in a lagoon provided a setting which gave it a unique beauty.

This setting has altered little since it was described by Don Juan da Castro, a Portuguese sea-captain who visited it in 1510:-

> "The situation of the city is in this manner: In the midst of a circular nook stands a flat island, almost perfectly round and level with the water, about a mile in compass. In this space there is not a foot of ground but what is taken up with houses; so that all the island is a city, and all the city an island. This is Suakem.
> On the East, South-East and South-West, its distance from the land is not over a bow-shot. The road for ships lies round about the city to the distance of a great cross-bow-shot; having every-where six or seven fathom of water, so that ships may cast anchor at pleasure, in a mud bottom. This road is encompassed with a great shoal, and that by others, which render it almost inaccessible by sea."

There are three islands in the Suakin lagoon but only one of them was ever fully built-up. The other two have

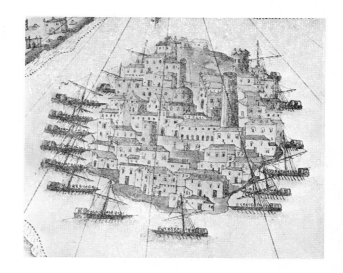

supported a few buildings from time to time. One is still occupied by the quarantine installations for pilgrims to Mecca; the other, called Condenser Island by the troops who occupied it in the campaigns of 1885-1896, is now devoid of any complete structure. For many years the gaunt, condenser-chimney towered up like a slim obelisk, a landmark for miles around, but it has now disappeared.

The third island, on which the main town was built, has been continuously inhabited for at least five hundred years and probably much longer. It is about 400 metres across and rather more than that in length.

The town was not planned; it grew up like most old towns with irregular, narrow streets and small clearings between blocks of houses of varying size and shape. There must have been close on three hundred buildings still intact up till the 1930's, but by 1940-50, when this survey was completed, a bare fifty remained, of which not more than a dozen were comparatively intact. The rest had either fallen down or been deliberately pulled down to provide lime or building-material for local needs on the mainland.

The *Geyf* or mainland-town is a separate entity encircled by fortifications built by Colonel Kitchener in the 1890's and provided with an impressive fortified gateway which is still standing and comparatively intact.

The main street, leading to the Causeway across to the island is gently curved and dominated on the left by the tall minaret of Shennawi Bey's mosque. Further

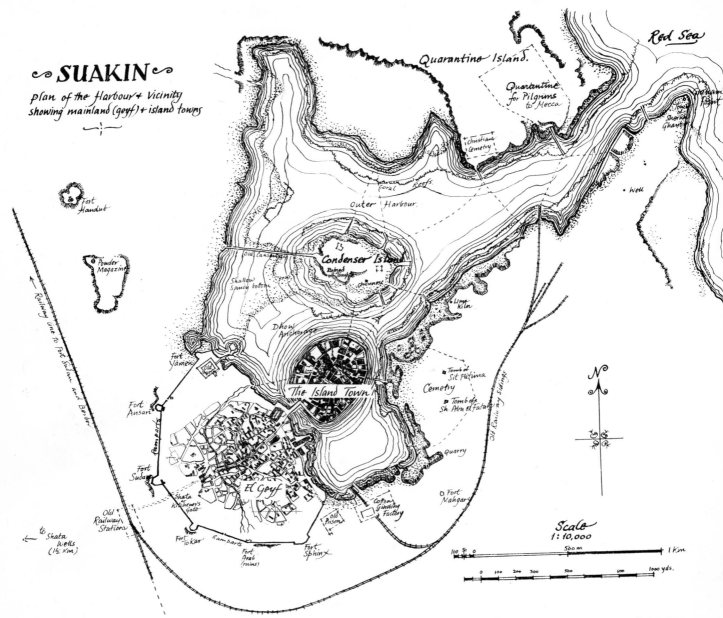

Red Sea

Quarantine Island.

Quarantine
for Pilgrims
to Mecca

Christian Cemetery

Coral Reefs

Outer Harbour

Well

Fort Handub

Powder Magazine

Old Causeway

Condenser Island

Ruined

Chimney

Lime Kiln

Shallow Sandy bottom

Dhow Anchorage

Fort Yameic

Old

Fort Ansari

Rampart

The Island Town

Tomb of Sit Fatima

Cemetery

Tomb of Sh. Abu el Fatah

Old Railway Sidings

Fort Sudan

Shata Kitchener's Gate

El Geyf

Old Prison

Cotton Ginning Factory

Quarry

Fort Mahgar

Railway line to Port Sudan and Berber

to Shata Wells (1½ Km)

Old Railway Station

Fort Tokar

Ramparts

Fort Arab (ruins)

Fort Sphinx

N

Scale
1:10,000

100 50 0 .... 500 m .... 1 Km

0 100 200 300 500 .... 1000 yds.

---

northwards, on the same side of the street, the fine mosque of Sayed Osman Mohammed Taj el Sir, with its two-balconied minaret and domed mausoleum, stands out above the surrounding houses and, beyond it stands the house of the Sharifa Miryam his widow. On the corner, by the Causeway leading to the island was the now ruined Wakala or caravanserai of Shennawi Bey, next to and dwarfing the Magedi Mosque, reputed to be the oldest mosque in Suakin.

There are a few more interesting old buildings on the

Geyf surrounded by the shanties, shops and drinking-houses of the mainly Hadendowah inhabitants; the large Musai Zawia (p. 64) with its fine dome and the modest three-arched Magzoubi Zawia (p. 63).

The fine house built by the Sharifa Miryam (p. 36) widow of Sayed Taj el Sir and chief representative of the Mirghanist Sect in the Eastern Sudan after his death, is empty but maintained in good condition by her family. It is near her late husband's mosque. Her other houses on the Island-Town have crumbled away.

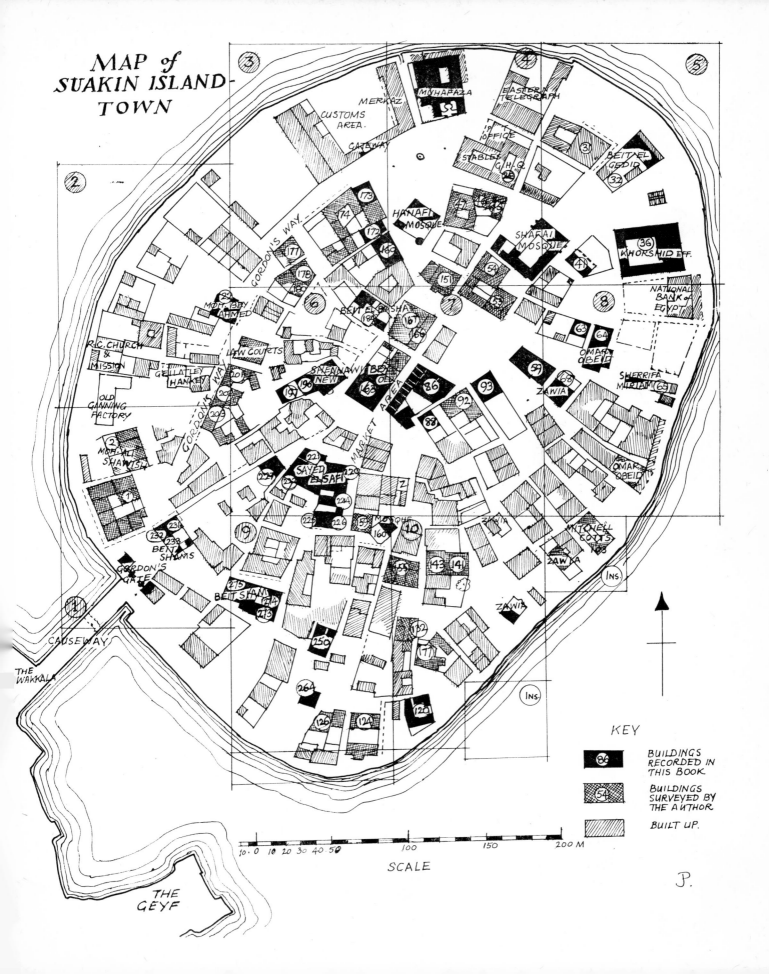

MAP of SUAKIN ISLAND TOWN

③ ④ ⑤

MERKAZ

CUSTOMS AREA.

MUHAFAZA

51

EASTERN TELEGRAPH

GATEWAY

② POST OFFICE

STABLES

G.H.Q. 35

③ ③1

BEIT EL GEDID 32

173

14 172

HANAFI MOSQUE

47

171

166

SHAFAI MOSQUE

41

(36) KHORSHID EFF.

178 180

54

151

MOH. BEY AHMED 29

⑥ BEIT EL BASHA 184

167 166

⑦

53

⑧

NATIONAL BANK of EGYPT

R.C.CHURCH & MISSION

LAW COURTS

100

SHENNAWY BEY OBEID

63 64

OMAR OBEID

GEILATLEY HANKEY

208 209 205

197 196

182

86

93 92

59

68 ZAWIA

SHERRIFA MIRIAM 65

OLD GINNING FACTORY

88

MOH. ALI SHAWISH 2

221

224 223

SAYED EL SAFI

220

7 162

Z

ZAWIA

MITCHELL COTTS 108

232 238 231 BEIT SHAMS

229 126

5 160

MOSQUE

12

ZAWIA

GORDON'S GATE

⑨

155

143 141

ZAWIA

INS

275 BEIT SHAMS 214 219

132

77

ZAWIA

CAUSEWAY

250

THE WAKKALA

264

INS

126 124 120

THE GEYF

KEY

86	BUILDINGS RECORDED IN THIS BOOK
54	BUILDINGS SURVEYED BY THE AUTHOR
	BUILT UP.

10 0 10 20 30 40 50   100   150   200 M

SCALE

P.

There are some 19th century buildings of lesser interest: the two-storeyed school; the Police Barracks; the Ginning-Factory, Prison and remains of the old Suakin-Berber Railway installations and the forts on the fortified wall.

There is also the beautiful little *Gubba*, the domed tomb of a local holy man, Sheikh Abul Fatah (p. 69) and the tombs of Sitt Fatima and Sheikh Gharib, the latter way out on the tip of the mainland called Graham's Point.

The Island-Town is reached by the Causeway built by General Gordon in 1877. One passes through his picturesque gateway (p. 72) and proceeds by a comparatively broad street cut by Gordon which the author has called "Gordon's Way" in this book, to the Muhafaza, Markaz and Customs-Area on the northern tip of the island.

The lay-out of the rest of the Island-Town is roughly radial since, being small and almost perfectly oval, access to the sea was always immediate and near. The main axis of the island is the shopping-street which ran roughly north-east and south-west. When the Causeway was built, General Gordon opened up "Gordon's Way" for quick and easy access to the Muhafaza, by-passing the *suk*, or market-area.

One now walks up "Gordon's Way", once lined by small Egyptian-type houses, passing the ruins of Mohammed Bey Ahmed's house (No. 22) on the left. The shopping-axis of the town farther to the east, ran behind Shennawi Bey's house (163) with its back row of shops on one side and another row opposite on plot 86, to form the shopping street or *suk*. It continued North towards the newly-built quarter with Muhafaza, Bank and Eastern Telegraph, and southwards past Sayed el Safi's house (220), after which it turned westward towards the causeway and the *Geyf* at the southern end of the island, where we started from.

The earlier houses, with the exception of Khorshid's, were mostly built on the southern half of the island nearest the mainland and formed a rough diameter with their northern windows facing seawards to the north-east. A few other houses and mosques may have existed on the northern half, amongst them the buildings on the northern tip over which the Muhafaza was later built — Beit el Basha (184), Khorshid's house (35) and the Hanafi and Shafa'i mosques and probably a few scattered smaller houses. But this half was mainly built-up later with Egyptian-type houses, in the late 19th century (thereby blocking the northern sea-view from the rest of the town). These buildings included the top-storey of the Muhafaza, the cusoms sheds and Markaz, the Eastern Telegraph building, Mitchel Cotts, National Bank of Egypt, Kitchener's GHQ, Beit el Gedid and a host of smaller shops and stores.

In general, however, the Island-Town presented a fairly homogeneous appearance because of the uniform scale and local building-materials used. Walking about its streets was pleasant and shady. The narrow streets funnelled the sea-breezes into the heart of the town, into the *mashrabiyas* and through the numerous ventilators up the stair-shafts into each and every room.

The *mashrabiyas* also provided extra overhanging shade in the street below. The occasional empty plot formed a useful open space and the variety of street-widths and angles of inclination provided a series of vistas both inwards from the sea and outwards towards and beyond it.

Finally there was ample space all round the island to walk by the sea along the quays forming the whole of its circumference. There were several ferries to the mainland or Geyf, before the causeway was built and many continued even afterwards. The causeway enabled hand- and horse-drawn carts to enter the island and people no longer had to save the cost of a ferry by wading or swimming across from the mainland.

But, as we shall see in the historical chapter which follows, like many other Red Sea ports, Suakin owed its decline to the advent of the steamship and the changed trading conditions which it brought with it. The narrow, coral-lined access-channel and the dangerous reefs surrounding it were unsuitable for large ships and this, amongst other things, led to the building of Port Sudan only forty miles away. This gradually drew off all the trade. Now Suakin Island is little more than an area of rubble amongst which a few isolated house-cores and two dilapidated mosques stand out incongruously like survivals of a drastic bombardment.

The *Geyf*, on the other hand, has grown since the fishing and shell industries have been moved there from Port Sudan. Suakin as a town continues to exist. It is the old Island-Town whose inhabitants were wealthy merchants from Jedda, the Yemen, Aden and Hadaramout, Ethiopia and Eritrea, India, Egypt and Syria, which has disappeared.

CHAPTER TWO
THE STORY OF SUAKIN

THE DOCUMENTED history of Suakin[4] begins after the rise of Islam and the conquest of Egypt and Syria by the Arabs in 641 A.D. In 750, the son of the Caliph Marwan II fled southwards down the Nile after the assassination of his father, and made his way to Axum in Abyssinia via Suakin and Aqiq, and from then on the area along the Red Sea coast becomes the scene of frequent skirmishes between the Beja tribes and the Egyptians. The name *Suakin* may have originated some time between this date and 969 when it is mentioned by the envoys of the Turkish Sultan who were sent there to try and convert the Sudan to the Moslem Faith, it being at that time still a Christian kingdom. In 1172, Salah ed Din (Saladin) invaded Nubia and his capture of Jerusalem drew the attention of Europe to the Eastern Mediterranean.

In 1213 Suakin was reported by Yaqut to be still inhabited by Negro Christians and, two years later, the Sultan of Egypt sent an expedition against them for confiscating the property of Egyptian merchants who died in their territory. For the first time, therefore, the town came under the direct rule of Egypt, and about this time we have the first description of the place by four *ansars* from Mecca: "A small village inhabited by natives of the Hameg tribe"; this was in 1255.

Between the years 1048 and 1300 Suakin had a powerful rival in the Port of Aidhab, a few hundred miles north and nearer to Jedda. This rivalry came to an end with the fall of Aidhab, along with Jedda, as a result of misappropriation by their inhabitants of merchandise from Egypt destined for Mecca. From then on, Suakin became the principal port·for Egypt on the African coast of the Red Sea until the building of Port Sudan at the beginning of the present century.

In 1451 members of the *Ashraf*, descendants of the Prophet Mohammed, came from Mecca to the Sudan and settled in the east near Kassala. They lived part of the year at Suakin and Sinkat. Some houses there still belong to the family. (Nos. 66 and 93 on the Island, and one on the mainland).

With the fall of Constantinople in 1453, the rise of the Ottoman Turks and the consequent eclipse of Egypt as a great power, Suakin and Jedda enjoyed a short period of independence and prosperity, providing a safer route for pilgrims to Mecca than the now unsafe northern route through Egypt. Then, in the 16th century, two new factors intervened; first, the Portuguese sailed round the Cape, up the coast of Africa and settled amongst the Abyssinians and, second, Amara Dunkas founded his Funj Kingdom in the Eastern Sudan, based on Sennar.

The Funj annexed Suakin, but their hold on it was never very firm. The Turks conquered Egypt in 1516, and when, a few years afterwards, they sent expeditions south to occupy Massawa, Suakin and Jedda, the Funj representatives fled.

From then on Suakin was, almost without interruption, under Turkish authority. The foundations, if not the super-structure, of many of its houses may date from this period. The Turks improved and enlarged the port, built houses of coral rock and left a Pasha there with a small force. The oldest reputed house on the island, called Beit el Basha (No. 184) may well have been occupied by him. It is however hardly grand enough to have housed a Turkish Pasha except at the very foundation of an outpost of a new dominion. (See description on p. 22).

In 1540 the Portuguese fleet under Stefano da Gama anchored in the bay on their way to attack the Turks at Suez. They quarrelled with the Governor, however, and sacked the town, an action which cost them dear, for news of it warned the Turks of their approach and, when they sailed into Suez to burn the Turkish fleet, they found the boats beached and were beaten back without even gaining a foothold. They eventually retired to Abyssinia and consolidated their position on the Indian Ocean.

Suakin next served as a base for the Turkish invasion of the Yemen in 1629, during which time larger and better houses may have been built.

The foundations at least of the larger old houses, notably that of Khorshid Effendi (No. 35) and possibly even that of Shennawi Bey (No. 163), could reasonably be dated from this period.

During the seventeenth and eighteenth centuries the Turks continued to exercise nominal control of Suakin, but their harsh and extortionate methods made their position precarious, with the result that, combined with the danger of Turkish pirates, and the newly-discovered Cape route to the Far East, the Red Sea in general, and Suakin in particular, suffered a period of decline, and when Lord Valentia visited it in 1805 he described the town as "nearly in ruins". This should not be taken too literally for he continues: "two minars gave it a handsome appearance, at a distance, the buildings . . . look much better than they really are. It covers the whole of the small island as it did in the days of da Castro . . . ". The two minarets referred to still stand today, and there seems little reason why they should not have been standing in the time of da Castro. The tower in his drawing could be interpreted to represen ta minaret (p. 9).

Burckhardt also visited Suakin and estimates that there were six hundred houses on the island, two thirds of which were falling into ruins, but the *Geyf*, or settlement on the mainland, was increasing in size and, as today, was larger than the Island-Town.

The firman from the Sultan of Turkey to the Khedive Ismail in 1865 gave his sons the right of accession, and granted to Egypt the ports of Massawa and Suakin in return for an additional yearly tribute.

As the only port of the Sudan, Suakin was of great value to Egypt. In addition, it was centrally placed for trade coming to Egypt from India, Abyssinia, Arabia and the Yemen, and was the main port for Sudanese and West African pilgrims to Mecca. Egyptian enterprise, therefore, developed the resources of the port as far as it was able, and during the next fifty years it rose steadily in importance.

Mumtaz Pasha became the first governor of the port and took up his appointment early in 1866. He enlarged many houses on the island, built new ones, and repaired others. The Muhafaza is the most noted of those which were enlarged by him. The top storey dates from this period (p. 72).

Egyptian merchants now settled in Suakin and built themselves large houses on the island. Once built, they were seldom repaired for their owners had not the money to pay for their upkeep. The result was that they soon became as unsafe as the money that had been loaned for their construction.

In 1869 Baker visited Suakin and noted that the population was only eight thousand, considerably less than it was stated to have been in the times prior to the Egyptian occupation. He came in an Egyptian sloop of war and stayed with Mumtaz Pasha. In the same year the Suez Canal was opened, and the Red Sea, instead of being a side-road for maritime commerce, became the Highway to the East. Suakin was bound to increase in importance under these new conditions, and it was not long before European merchants as well as Egyptians settled in the port.

Wylde,[5] who was at Aden in 1874, mentions that the merchants at Suakin and Massawa were simply the receiving and forwarding agents for the mercantile houses at Jedda, and that their only trade was, to all intents and purposes, the slave trade, supplying indirectly Cairo and Constantinople. Of honest trading there was a limited amount, but the demand for slaves knew no bounds, and even the highest government-officials filled their pockets with the profits of a trade which the Khedive had promised to stamp out.

The other exports from Suakin at this period were much the same as in the past: ivory and gum, coffee from Abyssinia, gold from Sennar, senna and ostrich feathers from Darfur and Kordofan, hides from Kassala; cotton, sesame-oil, and cattle from the local tribes. The imports naturally increased and included a large number of European goods such as sugar, candles, soap, rice, cloth from Manchester, cutlery and metal goods from Birmingham. These goods, received at Suakin, were forwarded by camel-caravans to Berber and Kassala, which were the two great distributing centres for Abyssinia and the Sudan. These caravans for the interior left Suakin about every three months; and after the construction of the Wakala, they loaded up outside this building, watched by a large crowd. Each caravan consisted of between five hundred and a thousand camels and its departure was one of the sights of the town.

Screw steamers were in operation between the ports of the Red Sea in 1874. Gessi arrived at Suakin on the *Zagazig* in April of that year. Travellers had difficulty in getting a vessel that would call there, as there was no certainty of obtaining any cargo for the return journey. But with the increased demand for foreign goods, and the greater possibilities of trading the produce of the country, conditions improved gradually and between 1874 and 1883 Suakin rose steadily in wealth. With this increase of European trade, more and more goods passed through Suakin instead of going through Egypt.

The Governor, European and Egyptian government officials, and chief merchants lived on the island. On the

Geyf, were the native quarters and the market, one street of which was taken up entirely with hairdressers' shops for the Beja tribesmen.

In 1877, General Gordon was appointed Governor-General of the Sudan, and on his way to Khartoum passed through Suakin. He ordered the building of the causeway between the island and the mainland, and this was completed in the first half of the following year, being built entirely by convict labour.

In 1881 the Egyptian decree declared the Eastern Sudan a separate province with a Governor-General of its own, independent of the rest of the Sudan. Ali ed Din was appointed the new Governor-General and took up his post early in 1882.

In June 1883 an Egyptian commission considered the question of a Sudan railway. Briefly, three routes were under consideration:

1. Suakin-Kassala-Goz Rejab-Khartoum,
2. Cairo, up the Nile, to Khartoum,
3. Suakin-Berber-Khartoum,

That the railway was never built was not the fault of the commission that recommended it. The growing unrest in the country gradually spread; and, through the activities of Osman Digna, eventually reached the Eastern Sudan.

The Madhist insurrection began around El Obeid in the Western Sudan about 1880 and moved rapidly eastwards to Khartoum and beyond to the Red Sea Hills. The Mahdists established their camp-town of Omdurman; it became a permanent and very populated town on the Nile bank opposite the capital which soon came under a state of siege. Khartoum's stand under General Gordon and its fall in 1885 is one of the most famous pages of nineteenth-century history and need not be repeated here, but the struggle in the East began to affect Suakin directly.

In his first few battles, Osman Digna was defeated and his prestige suffered to such an extent that he was scarcely able to collect together enough men to continue the fight. But the ambushing and annihilation on their way to Sinkat of Suleiman Pasha Nyaszi's garrison in November 1883, augmented Osman Digna's prestige and he was joined by the Kadi and other notables from Suakin. He then advanced on Tokar.

In the following year he killed over half of General Baker's four thousand reinforcements from Egypt at the battle of El Teb and successfully stormed the town of Sinkat. Further reinforcements, including British troops, however, defeated him at Tamai after a stiff resistance when the Beja tribesmen won renown by breaking a British Square.

For a time the port assumed a peaceful appearance, but Osman Digna took up the offensive again later in the year, the town was besieged and fired on during the night causing occasional casualties amongst the inhabitants.

In 1885, the year of the fall of Khartoum and the death of General Gordon, Suakin was already the base of the second expeditionary force consisting of thirteen thousand troops, which aimed not only at crushing Osman Digna but at building the Berber-Suakin Railway. The expedition was so badly organised and harrassed by the Dervishes[6] that it failed as ingloriously as the first and was withdrawn in April. In spite of the death of the Mahdi in July, Osman Digna was again besieging Suakin, having gained considerably in prestige and self-confidence and having cost the British Government £3,345,483 of fruitless expenditure. A skeleton garrison remained behind, and an uneasy tension reigned for nearly two years.

The Suakin merchants were not averse to trading with the enemy during this period. Under the Governor-Generalship of Colonel Kitchener, however, the route to Berber was made safe for caravans to proceed once more into the interior and trade returned to almost peace-time prosperity.

During his term of office, Kitchener completely remodelled the defences of the town, replacing the protective earth-wall with a twelve-foot brick one and building the present gate and six forts. He installed himself in the Muhafaza with his headquarters, while his Military Staff lived in a new house immediately behind the Post Office.[7]

1889 was a disastrous year for the Dervishes who lost more men by disease and famine than by war itself, and Osman Digna found himself almost deserted. Two successful operations by the British garrison in 1890 and 1891, in which Tokar was recaptured, obliged him to withdraw into the hills for a time, and Suakin was again left in peace, though bereft of its trade and under martial law.

In 1897 the Egyptian Army began to advance down the Nile. In September the troops occupied Berber. This finally decided the Beja tribes who, one and all, came over to the side of the Government, at any rate nominally. The Governor of Suakin became the Governor of the Red Sea Littoral, in fact as well as in name, and the Suakin-Berber road was once more open to trade.

A year later Omdurman fell and the Dervish rule over the Sudan was ended.

With the passing of the Sudan into British and Egyptian hands in 1898, the possibilities of developing Suakin as the only available port were thoroughly investigated. The town and harbour presented many problems. The harbour entrance was narrow, tortuous and difficult for large vessels. The water-supply was poor and inadequate. The buildings were in a bad state of repair and a new quarter would have to be found for the European population which would settle there sooner or later.

Suggestions were put forward for rebuilding in 1903. Graham's Point (see map p. 10) was thought to be the only possible site for a European quarter. A quay was to be constructed along the south side of the harbour near the proposed site of the new town, and a railway terminus was also to be built there. Both the island and the mainland quarters would need replanning and rebuilding.

In 1904, Colonel Ralston Kennedy of the Public-Works Department made a report, more than half of which consisted in proving how much more suitable a site for the port was the harbour of Mersa Barghout,

some forty miles to the north. Eventually it was decided to abandon the proposed changes at Suakin and build a completely new port at Mersa Barghout.

But the new port was yet to be built, and for a short period Suakin continued to flourish. A railway was built from Atbara in 1905 and extended to Port Sudan, as the new harbour was called, the following January. For a time all the trade continued to come through Suakin, The National Bank of Egypt, The Eastern Telegraph Company, shipping companies and business firms all had their offices there. The Government officials and other Europeans lived on the island in the old houses. There was a club and games and other social activities were organised.

The Province-Headquarters were transferred to Port Sudan in 1910, a year after the new port had been opened by the Khedive of Egypt. But trade could not be transferred there so easily and for some years Suakin was still the main port for the country. The Great War held up the development of Port Sudan and further prolonged the life of Suakin. It was not until 1922 that all the important businesses had finally deserted the old port for the new. Since that period Suakin has rapidly fallen into ruin through disuse. The piers had disappeared by 1936, the jetties crumbled away into the reefs along the sides of the harbour, and no more large ships entered the old port.[8] To-day it is mostly rubble and the exterior walls of all the houses have fallen down.

THE MURJAIHA: MERRY-GO-ROUND.

CHAPTER THREE
DOMESTIC LIFE IN SUAKIN

BEFORE examining the houses themselves it would be as well to have a clear idea of the kind of life they were intended for. While houses in the Western World to-day are divided according to functions, for privacy with bedrooms, dining-rooms, sitting-rooms, play-rooms, studies and so-on, Moslem, and oriental houses in general, provide for more people at a time and are divided into social categories. First, private and public, then the former further divided according to the member of the family, each branch with its independent quarters. When the house can no longer accommodate them, another house is built on the same or an adjacent plot and sometimes these grow to become many inter-connecting houses, to form a family neighbourhood-unit.

There is a clear distinction between private and social life in a Moslem family and contact with strangers is more distant and formal than in the West to-day. The house is divided into two parts: on the ground floor, a smaller but usually more imposing part for the reception and entertainment of guests, called in Turkish, the *salaamlik*; and the larger, upper part of the house which is occupied by the family, the women and children, which is called the *harim*. This is always the most extensive part since it has to cater, not only for one or two wives and their offspring, but a varying number of women relatives, grandmothers, aunts and sisters, visitors and their children, not to mention the maid-servants. The *harim* in Suakin consisted of a series of suites or sitting-rooms each called a *majlis* (plural *majalis*). These often had a smaller room, called the *khazana*, adjoining the larger and communicating with it, and an independent cooking-area, washing-space with a water-jar or *zeer*, a latrine and a store. Each suite would be occupied by one branch of the family, a wife, mother-in-law, or widowed aunt, and their respective children and maid-servants. Family distinctions were not strict and the women and children would 'doss down' to sleep almost anywhere on the carpeted seats and floors or outside on the roof in their allotted terrace or *kharjah*. Children were not allowed into their father's bedroom before seven in the morning or between midday and three in the afternoon—or at night. A *majlis* might be re-allotted on the arrival into the house of a newly-married couple.

The *salaamlik* on the ground-floor consisted of a large reception-room, smaller adjoining room, latrine and store. People lived on the upper floors which were safer, more private and where there was more light and the air cleaner. There was an entrance-lobby called a *dihlis*, which sometimes had an imposing reception end or *diwan*. The latter was composed of two parts, a lower, uncarpeted portion in which shoes were left; the other half was raised up a step and carpeted. This contained platform-seats or a *maga'ad* all round it and about 50 cm. from the ground on which one could sit cross-legged and there would also be a *mashrabiya* to sit and sleep in. (The many uses of the *mashrabiya* are described on p. 21). A large house might also have a smaller guest-room giving off the *diwan*. (see House 163, p. 29).

SLEEPING

The top storey and roof contained terraces called *kharjas* for sleeping out at night, one for the owner and his wife, the other for the rest of the family with an adjoining shaded portion, a *sala* or *darwah* or, in some cases, a *majlis*, store and latrine. Sleeping was on cord-strung beds called *angareebs* which have been in use in Egypt and the Sudan since Pharaonic times. There were sometimes a large kitchen-area and various store-rooms on the top floor. The servants usually slept downstairs and even outside at night.

ENTRANCES

There were usually two entrances to the house, one for the womenfolk, the other for the men and visitors. Occasionally the upper floors of houses communicated; in two instances there was even a bridge (*mamurr*) across the street for the members of the *harim* (probably related) to meet without going outside. (see p. 46) Women did not appear at social functions but in the larger houses they could watch from specially placed windows upstairs. An example was to be seen in the house of Shennawi Bey (No. 163, p. 32) and in many houses in Jedda and Cairo.

FEEDING

The eating-customs of Moslems make for great

simplicity in catering and receiving unexpected extra numbers, and meal-times are not fixed. The custom of sitting cross-legged on carpets and eating communally from a large tray dispenses with the need for tables and chairs. Eating with the fingers dispenses with all cutlery save large spoons for soup. The only utensils required are bowls and dishes brought on a tray and placed on the floor. If, however, room for more people is required another tray is brought in. All left-overs are eaten by the family and servants — there is very little waste.

When finished with, bowls, trays or coffee-jugs, mostly handmade and decorative in themselves, were placed on the recessed shelves with which each room was provided, for display, much as kitchen-dressers did in Europe. Storage-space was thus combined with display.

FURNITURE

Eastern peoples, though they did not sit on chairs, never sat directly on the ground or on a bare floor but on rugs, mats or skins. In houses the rugs were spread on both floor and *maga'ad* platforms, the former for walking on barefoot and the latter for sitting and sleeping on. These *maga'ads* (also called *karaweit*) were made of wood; similar seats made of earth or stone on the ground-floor and outside are called *mastabas*. They are about a metre wide, to take the legs folded, and are therefore too wide and too high to sit on comfortably with legs dangling. In hot countries it is more comfortable to keep feet on the same level as the body. *Maga'ads* and *roshans* are provided with cushions called *masnads*. Tight little bolsters called *makhaddas* can be placed across the *karaweits* to form a head-rest when lying down or sleeping; they can also be put under the armpits or in the small of the back for comfort in reclining. The *maga'ads* also serve as beds and four people could comfortably lie down in a room no more than three metres square. Such a room, which is small by Sudanese standards, appeared quite spacious in Suakin because it was empty of furniture and people sat mostly in the *mashrabiya* (p. 21).

In the *harim* the entire floor was carpeted or covered with mats and, since everyone walked about barefoot, the room was really like a large couch and one could sit, lie or walk about it as one pleased. Windows, *mashrabiyas* and the sills of recessed shelves were nearer the floor in these upper rooms.

COOKING

Kitchen requirements, too, were characteristically simple. They contained a small cooking-range raised about 35 cm. from the floor with three or four grated fire-holes. Wood charcoal was the fuel used, and it was stored in a large recess upstairs with reserves in a larger store under the ground-floor stairs. The person cooking sat on a low stool with her pots, pans and dishes around her on trays and palm-frond mats on the floor. Food was not served piping-hot as in Europe; instead it was highly seasoned with peppers and spices. It did not easily congeal and left-overs could be warmed-up again.

WASHING

Washing and bathing were simplified rather than complicated by the fact that Moslems will not, on principle, wash in still water. Even to wash their hands the water must be poured from a cup or bowl. In Suakin, where the sea was but a few yards away, there was little need for elaborate indoor bathing arrangements. A small bathing-space with a drained floor, a low stool, a large earthenware jar or *zeer*, with a wide mouth in which to dip a small bowl or *calabash*, a ledge for soap and *lufah*[9] is all that was required. The *zeer* maintains water at a temperature noticeably cooler than the surrounding atmosphere, and the bathwaste also served to flush the latrine which adjoined it. The latter consisted of a hole in the floor above a shaft built into the thickness of the wall down to a pit below. There was usually one for each *majlis* and *diwan*.

STORAGE

Belongings were stored in three ways: bulky objects like saddles, sacks of produce, boxes etc. were kept in the store-rooms on the ground-floor and occasionally on an upper floor; clothes, blankets and hangings would lie in decorated wooden chests which helped to furnish the otherwise empty rooms. Clothes, being loose-fitting and light, did not need to be kept hanging in wardrobes. The third method of keeping small things was in the recessed shelves or *rufuf* already mentioned; some of these had doors converting them into built-in cupboards. These were carefully placed for symmetry on either side of windows or in threes on an otherwise blank wall. In these, smaller objects like lamps, trinket-boxes, coffee-jugs, cups and water-jugs were placed.

LIGHTING

Lighting was by oil-lamps and, though in the West to-day this would seem dim, such a light is no disadvantage for making conversation. In the larger rooms lanterns were hung from a hook at the top of a dividing-arch, in the centre of the ceiling, or in the centre of the *mashrabiya*. Little portable oil-lamps were also placed in niches at appropriate places: at the sides of a *mashrabiya*, near an entrance-door or half-way up a flight of stairs. The inhabitants of Suakin lived by the sun (and moon) and made full use of this natural light for their work and recreation. The nights in the tropics come as a welcome relief from the bright glare and heat of the day; almost half of each month is moonlit and then life goes on into the early hours of the morning.

STREET-LIGHTING

While on the subject of lighting, in Suakin there was a system of street-lighting by oil-lamps held by brackets at street-corners. These were lit and maintained by the night-watchmen, three in number, who would call out to each-other during the night; "Number One", "Number Two", "Number Three". Failure to reply implied that the watchman was asleep and he would be reported to the Mamur in the morning. There was also considerable rowing about the lagoon in boats and the white lamp-lit town floating on its island-raft reflected in the water must have presented a pleasant sight.

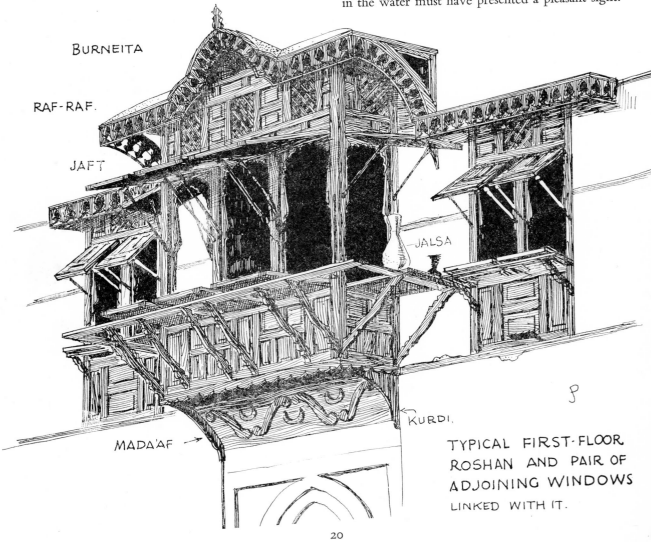

BURNEITA

RAF-RAF.

JAFT

JALSA

MADA'AF →

← KURDI.

TYPICAL FIRST-FLOOR ROSHAN AND PAIR OF ADJOINING WINDOWS LINKED WITH IT.

CHAPTER FOUR
ROSHANS: CASEMENT WINDOWS

THE DISTINGUISHING external features of the old houses of the Red Sea and some other Islamic and Indian styles are the large casement-windows jutting-out into the street to catch the slightest passing breeze. In Egypt they are called *mashrabiyas*, but in Suakin and Jedda they were known as *roshans*. They were the focal point of life within a room as well as the main feature of the house from without. At least one of these impressive pieces of woodwork was found in every living-room; many had two and occasionally there were three.[10]

Most living-rooms were situated in the north-east or north-west corner of the house. These rooms were the coolest, having a *roshan* in each of the two outside walls, north and west or north and east. In this way one of them was bound to receive the prevailing breeze and much of the available shade; the south side of a house seldom had living-accommodation but was reserved for staircases, stores and latrines.

The *roshans* of Suakin and Jedda were made of solid Java teak, called *jawi*, shipped direct from the East Indies, for even heavy teak is a safe cargo in small sailing craft. In Jedda some houses have one or two sides almost entirely encased in woodwork, windows and *roshans* often being joined together, horizontally, by shades and balconies or, vertically, by wooden corniced crowns of the lower *roshan* supporting the bottom of the upper one at the same time.

The *roshan* can be traced as far east as India and, westwards, there are some superb *roshans* on the Town-Hall of Lima in Peru, made on eastern models by the Spaniards; they are familiar in southern Spain and a similar feature built in masonry is common in Malta and many coastal towns in the Peleponnese. *Roshans* are also found in Massawa and Somalia. The European bay-window is a kind of *roshan* existing to catch the *light* rather than the breeze.

The size of a *roshan* is related to the dimensions of the human body; it is wide enough to lie down in comfortably, that is just over two metres, 2.40 m. usually; high enough to stand in, about 3 metres, and projecting about 60 cm. into the street. Inside, if we add 60-80 cm. for the thickness of the wall, it makes a carpeted alcove about 2.40 m. wide by 1.20-1.40 m. deep, a space in which two or three people can sit around a coffee-tray or

hookah[11] in comfort. The *maga'ad* within the room is flush with the bottom of the *roshan* and adds about a metre to its depth, bringing it into the room.

The lower portion is panelled to a height of about 50 cm. Seated on the *roshan* floor, one can lean over this lower part and see into the street. This and the open portion above is called the *jalsa;* it is divided horizontally into two unequal sets of shutters which close the openings. The shutters are hinged at top and bottom and swing outwards; the larger top ones form an extra shade, the smaller lower ones are supported by brackets outside called *mada'af* to make a ledge.

The upper shutters are held open by long, metal hooks which act as stays; when shut, the lower shutters are held in place by small hooks to prevent them falling open outwards. These are illustrated on p. 109.

On the ground-floor *roshans*, barred for security, sliding sash panels were used instead of hinged ones. Sash-type panels were sometimes also used in upper *roshans* and occasionally sliding *shish* or trellised panels were used as well as wooden panelled shutters. (No. 226).

Sometimes, again, basket-like trellis screens were added to the *mada'af* outside the *roshan* when there was the likelihood of being overlooked. They are common and necessary in a large town like Jedda but greatly mar the appearance of the *roshan* itself. They were found in a few houses in Suakin, notably Beit Siam (No. 275) and Beit Ali Shawish (No. 2).

Above the open *jalsa* there was another, panelled portion in which ventilating grilles were inserted. The elements of a *roshan* can be varied in a number of ways, and except when a pair was made for symmetry, there are no two identical *roshans* in either Suakin or Jedda.

Roshans could be kept open at night for sleeping in coolness. They were lit either by a lantern suspended from the *roshan*'s own ceiling or by little lamps placed in *tagas* let into the thickness of the wall at about shoulder-height when seated.

Most of the leisure-time was spent in the *roshans*, chatting, sipping coffee, smoking a *hookah*, eating, sleeping, or gazing at the seascape or the local pageantry of an oriental town with its frequent festivities, the arrival and departure of caravans and pilgrims to Mecca.

CHAPTER FIVE
EARLIER AND LARGER TURKISH HOUSES

THE BUILDINGS on the island fall into two groups; those built before 1860 which derived mainly from Jedda, and those built after that date which showed European influences from Egypt. Both kinds were built of the same local coral. Some houses were of mixed styles; the lower storey in Turkish and the upper ones in Egyptian style.

The Turkish houses and mosques of the first group were of the greater interest and occupy most of this book. They were in the same tradition as Mecca and Medina which must have remained constant for many centuries in a conservative culture such as that of Islam. This makes it difficult to date them with any accuracy. Beit el Basha (No. 184) or the Pasha's House, reputed by the local people to be the oldest house on the island, and the Magedi Mosque on the mainland could well date from the time of the Turkish occupation of Egypt in 1516. The decoration on the arch of the *diwan* was a well-known motif found on many of the old 16th/17th century palaces of Cairo. It is not unreasonable to suppose that a few houses could survive for four centuries on a site which has been continuously inhabited for much longer. The Magedi Mosque may be even older, for both this mosque and two of the houses resemble pre-thirteenth century buildings in size on the island of Iri farther down the Red Sea coast.

The remains on that island, now buried in sand, are described by Major Hebbert[12] as being about 25 metres square, higher on one side than the other three and containing a water-cistern for collecting rain-water in the middle. There are over eighty ruined water-cisterns in Iri, and there may have been more. Khorshid Effendi's house in Suakin is 30 metres square, higher on the north side and contains a cistern; Shennawi Bey's house, the next in date, is precisely 25 metres square and may well be built on an older foundation. It also contains a water-cistern.

A ruined mosque which Major Hebbert also excavated on Iri is identical in plan and dimensions with the Magedi Mosque still standing at Suakin (p. 65). According to Crowfoot, Iri was destroyed or abandoned in the thirteenth century.[13]

"Original Type" Houses (Nos. 41, 120 and 250)
If it is difficult to be certain of a true chronological sequence in the houses, it is possible to trace a logical development from a simple dwelling-unit of two or three rooms, which I have called "Original Type" houses to distinguish them from the more elaborate multi-storeyed buildings.

These small, single-storey houses are built in the same way as the larger houses and mosques and observe the same arrangement, proportions and dimensions in their rooms. They are normally 3.5 metres (6 *giddas*) wide and from 8 to 13 metres long according to whether they form a single room or a related pair of rooms. The smaller room of the pair was the family-quarters, the larger portion, the guest-room or general living-room. This arrangement resembles that of a Bedouin tent.

These little houses contained the characteristic details of the larger houses; recessed wall-shelves, arranged in threes with ventilators at the head of each; ornamented door-hoods, panelled doors and simple, undecorated lattice-work windows. There were dozens of such houses scattered among the taller buildings on both island and mainland. Some of the smaller mosques or *zawias* are little more than enlargements of these domestic houses. Because of their low height these buildings were less likely to collapse than the taller buildings and they, therefore, survived longer. Some of them could reasonably have been inhabited *before* the Turkish annexation in the early sixteenth century.

A single *majlis*-unit enclosed by a walled courtyard, or wooden fence, in which temporary wooden structures might be built would develop into a series of rooms surrounding part or all of the perimeter, for in the early days there would be room on the island to expand without building upwards. According to da Castro's drawing, (p. 9), there were some multi-storeyed houses on the island before 1510.

Beit El Basha (No. 184): "The Pasha's House"
This was the name given to the house by some of the inhabitants of Suakin. A small well-built and well-finished building, consisting of one ground-floor room with a second room above it, store and external

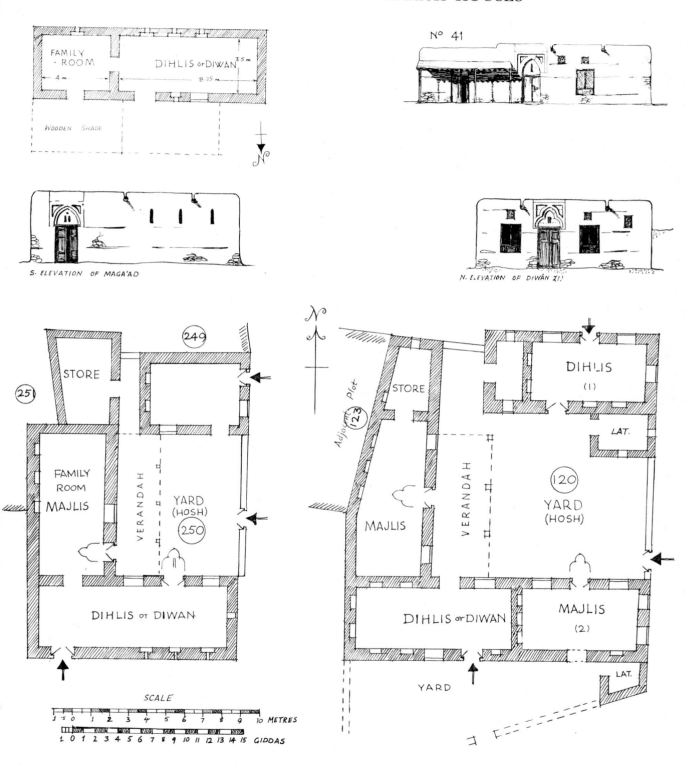

FAMILY ROOM

4 m

DIHLIS or DIWAN · 3·5 m

8·25

WOODEN SHADE

N

Nº 41

S· ELEVATION OF MAGA'AD

N. ELEVATION OF DIWÂN 21)

STORE (24)

(25)

FAMILY ROOM MAJLIS

VERANDAH

YARD (HOSH) (250)

DIHLIS or DIWAN

STORE

Adjacent Plot (123)

MAJLIS

VERANDAH

DIHLIS (1)

LAT.

(120) YARD (HOSH)

DIHLIS or DIWAN

MAJLIS (2)

YARD

LAT.

SCALE

5 0 1 2 3 4 5 6 7 8 9 10 METRES

0 1 2 3 4 5 6 7 8 9 10 11 12 13 14 15 GIDDAS

BEIT EL BASHA, No. 184

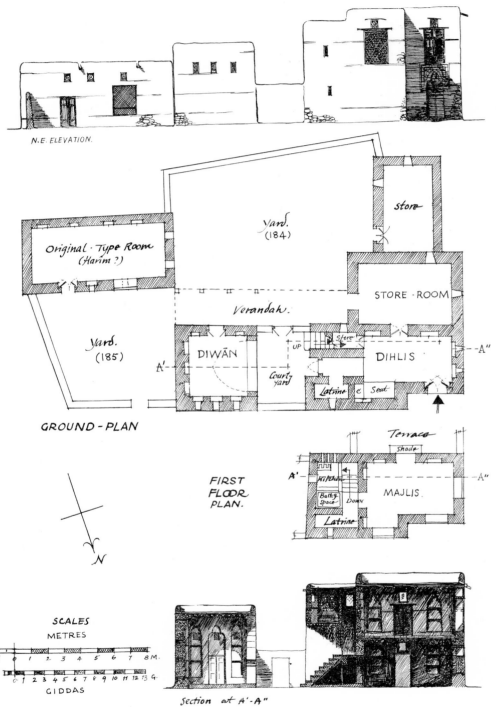

N.E. ELEVATION.

Yard.
(184)

Store

Original · Type Room
(Harim ?)

STORE · ROOM

Verandah.

Yard.
(185)

DIWĀN

UP

Store

DIHLIS

A'

A"

Court
yard

Latrine

Seat

GROUND - PLAN

FIRST
FLOOR
PLAN.

Terrace

Shade

A'

Kitchen

A"

Bathg
Space

Down

MAJLIS.

Latrine

N

SCALES
METRES
1 0 1 2 3 4 5 6 7 8 M.
0 1 2 3 4 5 6 7 8 9 10 11 12 13 G.
GIDDAS

Section at A'-A"

DIWAN IN
BEIT EL BASHA.

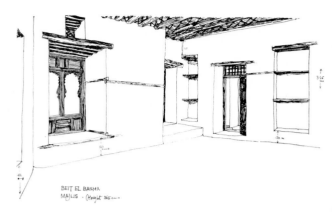

BEIT EL BASHA
MAJLIS · (Height 365 ·

BEIT EL BASHA, No. 184

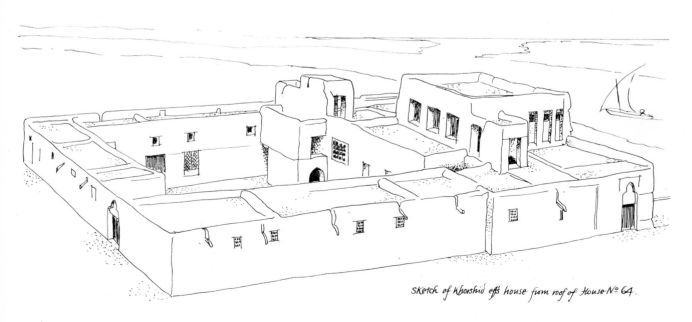

Sketch of Khorshid eff's house from roof of House Nº 64.

diwan. The latter had a carved stone fillet with a decorative motif found on the 16th-17th century mosques and palaces in Cairo.[14] It was an imposing, if small, outside reception-room. Beit el Basha may have been the house built for the Turkish Governor when the island was first taken over in 1518 or 1520. It was the kind of house one might expect from builders of an old-established tradition in an out-post of a newly acquired territory. On the other hand the Pasha referred to might be Mumtaz Pasha who might have had it built for himself before he added the upper storeys to the Muhafaza in 1866.

The lower of the two rooms, the *dihlis* (entrance-hall) through which access to the main *diwan* or sitting-room above could alone be obtained, had a carved door-hood (*'agd mawshah*) over a panelled door. The decorated back of the door alone (p. 117) was visible in 1950; the front had been boarded over. The room contained a store-cupboard under the stairs closed by a carved wooden door quite unlike the ones in the other houses; it was made of mahogany and not teak like most of the other woodwork in the town. The design was geometric and Islamic in character, whereas the carved doors in Jedda and others in Suakin had floral motifs which are of Indonesian origin. The room had a seat or *maga'ad* to sit on but no *roshan*. A door on the opposite side led into a larger room which may have been a store. Everything pointed to a house which was quite different from the other houses on the island, and that is another reason why I think it was earlier and possibly the earliest house apart from the undatable "original type" houses.

A narrow passage led from the *dihlis* to the inner courtyard and spacious *diwan* or open reception-room spanned by an archway on its open side. This arch was decorated with the carved stone fillet already mentioned. It would be here that the owner took his leisure and interviewed his visitors or petitioners.

A small stairway led from this courtyard up to the living-room above and a bathing and cooking-space half-way up. There may have been other ground-floor rooms of "original type" occupied by the family and servants, but the surviving part of the house when I saw it, was unique and independent. The upstairs room was spacious but had no *roshan*. If it was not an early house it becomes very difficult to explain its unusual character or why it was ever called "Beit el Basha".

Khorshid Effendi's House (No. 35)
This was a fine, single-storey house on the north-east side of the island. Its privileged position and its whole style lead me to think it was the next oldest house to Beit el Basha. It had many unique features not found in the other houses and was unlike them in lay-out and general appearance. It is like many of the houses illustrated in da Castro's drawing (p. 9).

It had a large and elaborately-decorated *diwan* higher than the remaining rooms. The latter were small and arranged round three sides of a large, square courtyard. The *diwan* itself occupied the fourth side. It may be traces of houses like this that Dr Hebbert found in Iri. (See p. 22).

The *diwan* approached a cube in form, being about 6 metres (10 *giddas*) square and about 4 to 5 metres high. It was spanned half-way across by a large pointed arch, halving the length of the beams. There was a large, deep *roshan* on the east side, quite unlike any other *roshan* on the island (or in Jedda for that matter). Apart from a dozen little ventilators high-up near the roof and two windows, this was the only source of light in the room, giving it a restful dimness and coolness. The walls were divided into a series of recesses or internal buttresses. The recesses contained doors, windows, and recessed shelves, some with panelled doors. They relieved the weight on lintels and the roof joists were mainly supported by the thicker parts of the wall.

The walls of the room were covered with geometric and floral arabesques incised in the plaster some of which have now been revealed for all to see since the collapse of the front wall of the house.

The floor of one half of the room was raised 60 cm. (1 *gidda*) above the other half and separated from it by a wooden balustrade. The upper half was completely carpeted and its three sides had continuous seating-platforms at the same level as the floor of the central *roshan*, called *karaweit*. The lower half of the room also had a *maga'ad* down one side, and a door leading into a large back room and the central courtyard of the house. The south wall had three high-placed clerestory windows, and was also decorated with incised patterns.

The general scale and appearance of this house and the presence of a unique *roshan* would make it different in date from Beit el Basha, but its large area and courtyard surrounded by single-storey rooms would seem to

FRONT (EAST) ELEVATION

UNFINISHED WING

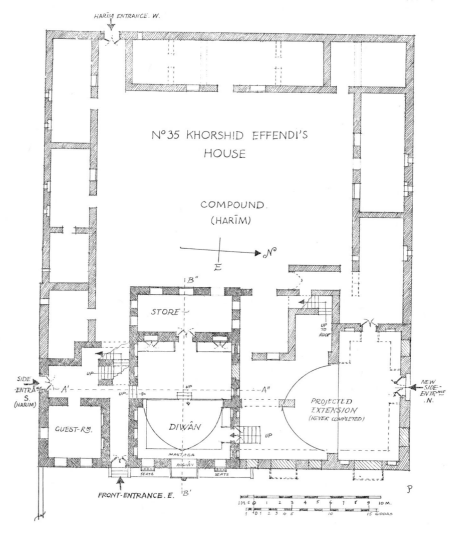

HARĪM ENTRANCE. W.

Nº 35 KHORSHID EFFENDI'S
HOUSE

COMPOUND.
(HARĪM)

Nº

E

STORE

B"

UP
TO
ROOF

SIDE
ENTRᴬ
S.
(HARĪM)

A'

A"

UP

UP

NEW
SIDE-
ENTᴿᴬᴺᶜᴱ
.N.

GUEST-Rᵐ.

PROJECTED
EXTENSION
(NEVER COMPLETED)

DIWÂN

UP

MASTABA
RUGWAY

SEATS

SEATS

FRONT-ENTRANCE. E.   B'

1M.5 0 1 2 3 4 5 6 7 8 9 10 M.

1 ½ 0 1 2 3 4 5   10   15 GIDDAS

KHORSHID'S DIWAN

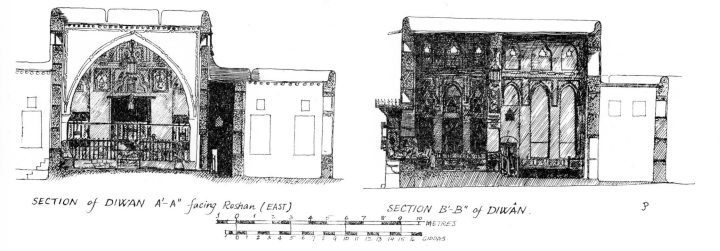

SECTION of DIWAN A'-A" facing Roshan (EAST)   SECTION B'-B" of DIWÂN.

imply a lavish use of land prior to any large-scale occupancy of the island.

The House of Shennawi Bey (No. 163)

This was a large, impressive three-storey building occupying a plot at the centre of the island. It showed a considerable development in design compared with the buildings so-far examined. It was a three-storeyed family-mansion built around a central light-well. It had four stairways, over twenty rooms and numerous alcoves and stores. It was a fully-developed example of the Red Sea style, typical of many others in Jedda, and is worth describing in some detail.

Ground Floor. The *salaamlik* was entered through the *dihlis* (entrance room) with a *mastaba* (stone seat) on one side and a small guest-room on the right. The latter looked onto the main *diwan* which occupied the south-west corner of the house. The rest of the floor was given up to stores and a row of lock-up shops forming the *suk* and running along the whole of the east side of the block. There was a central cistern underneath, re-calling the cisterns in the fourteenth-century houses on Iri.

The *diwan* was similar to many such in Jedda. It was divided into two portions by a pointed arch, and the *iwan*[15] or carpeted sitting-part was raised above the other part. Shoes would be left on the uncarpeted floor of the lower half. This portion, however, was two storeys high and had a high-placed arch opening onto the street, admitting light. In houses of this type in Jedda, this portion of the *diwan* is larger and often open

to the sky. The sitting part (*iwan*) was surrounded by the *karaweit* platforms and had a *roshan* on the west side (replaced by a doorway when the room was briefly turned into a museum in the 1940's) The south side had three recessed cupboards with carved wooden doors and high-placed ventilators (*tagas*). A door led from the east wall into a room which was probably used as a store.

In the lower half of the *diwan* there were three, open recessed shelves. At the level of the floor upstairs, three windows looked onto the *diwan* below. The dividing arch was decorated with an incised floral design similar to that in Khorshid's house (p. 28) while the rest of the room was picked-out with black pebbled decoration.

The upper floors, or harim, were divided into a number of independent suites of *majalis* arranged around a light-well. It is worth examining each of these quarters in turn.

Access to them was obtained by a small and un-obtrusive staircase, one of four stair-systems on the upper floors. There were four *majalis* on the first floor, the biggest of which was situated over the *diwan* on the hot, south-west corner; not a very suitable location for the main *majlis*, since its longest wall was on the south side. In consequence, it had no *roshans* on the side, but only one on the short west wall of the room and a flat window on the north side looking into the *diwan* below. It may have been to compensate for this rather poor main *majlis* that a larger suite was built on the top floor.

The three other *majalis*, one on the north-west corner and the two others over the shops on the east

29

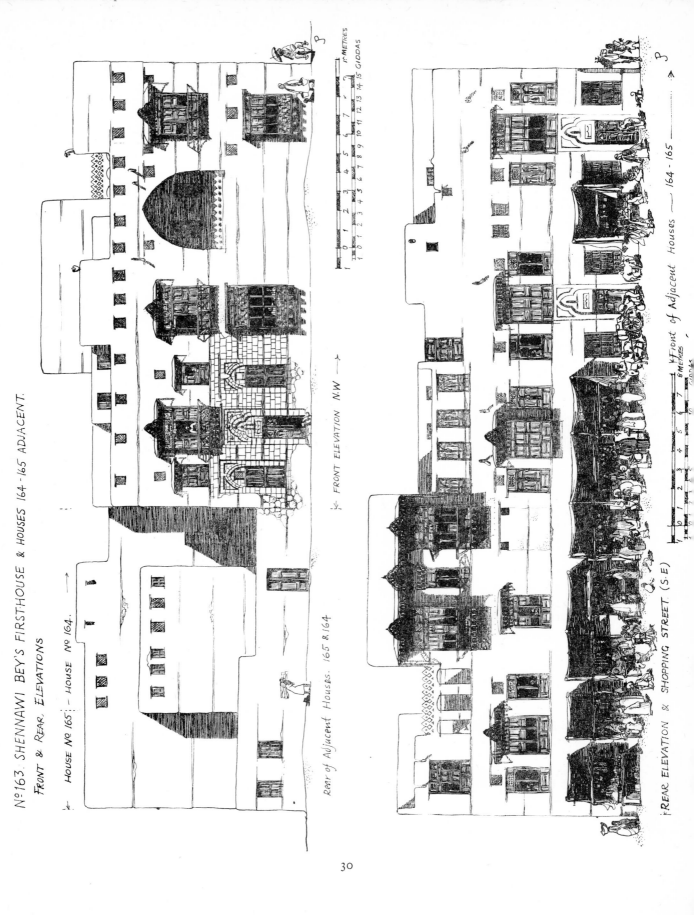

Nº163. SHENNAWI BEY'S FIRSTHOUSE & HOUSES 164-165 ADJACENT.

FRONT & REAR ELEVATIONS

← HOUSE Nº 165. ─ HOUSE Nº 164.

← FRONT ELEVATION N.W →

Rear of Adjacent Houses. 165 &164.

← REAR ELEVATION & SHOPPING STREET. (S.E)

Front of Adjacent Houses ─ 164-165 →

side, were less important. The north-west one had two *roshans*; the north-east one had only one, and that in the south-east corner *majlis*, none at all, but it had a small sleeping-terrace on the north side. From the plans one can see a complex system of stair-ways and numerous store-rooms, latrines and washing-spaces.

The top floor had two terraces or *kharjas* with shaded areas (*darwas*), each with an independent terrace, a large kitchen-area and the great *majlis* already referred to with its own access-stairway, terrace and separate store and latrine. The kitchen would have been a communal one; there were no separate kitchens in the rest of the house, but there are several little corners which could be used for cooking and where coffee could be brewed.

At the head of one of the staircases and in other strategically placed corners of the house, large porous water-jars or *zeers* were kept for coolness. From them the numerous smaller water-jars or *gullas*, standing in the *roshans* to cool, would be filled.

The last suite to be considered is the great *majlis* on the east side of the top storey. This room measured about 9 metres (15 *giddas*) by 5 metres and was divided in half by a carved wooden archway. It had a fine pair of *roshans* with a smaller projecting window between them for water-jars all under one large, ornamented wooden shade-hood (*raf-raf*). It also had its own terrace with windows and shelf-recesses and a separate store and latrine. This terrace or *kharja* was an open-air sleeping-place. The whole suite, carpeted and furnished, must have made a very pleasant living-quarter.

DIWAN IN THE HOUSE OF SHENNAWI BEY

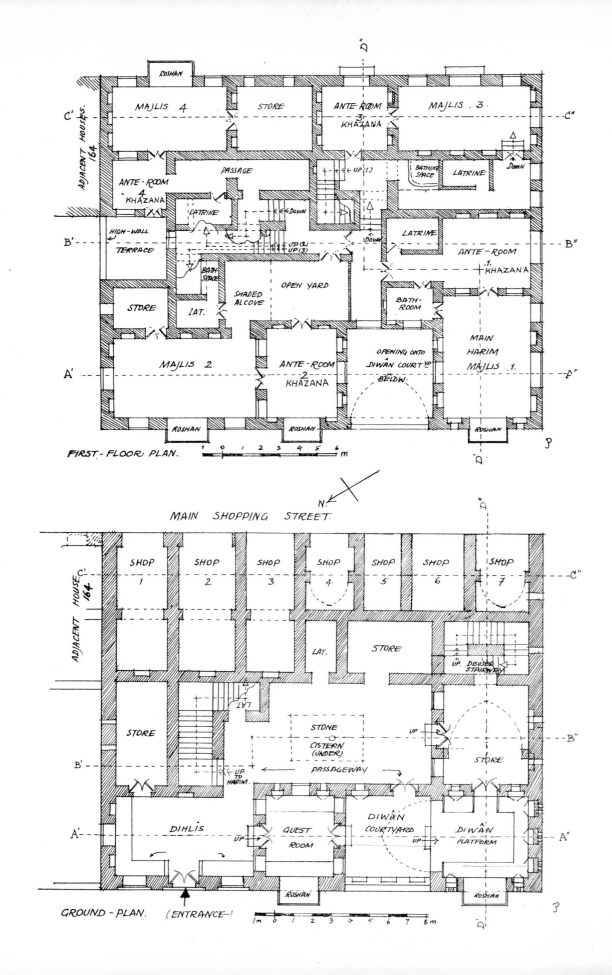

FIRST-FLOOR PLAN.

1 0 1 2 3 4 5 6 m

Labels in first-floor plan:
ROSHAN
MAJLIS 4 · STORE · ANTE-ROOM 3 KHAZANA · MAJLIS 3
C' ADJACENT HOUSES. 164 — C"
PASSAGE
ANTE-ROOM 4 KHAZANA
LATRINE
UP (1)
BATHING SPACE · LATRINE
Down
HIGH-WALL
TERRACE
LATRINE
Down
UP (2) UP (3)
Down
ANTE-ROOM 1 KHAZANA
B' — B"
BATH SPACE
SHADED ALCOVE
OPEN YARD
BATH-ROOM
STORE · LAT.
MAJLIS 2 · ANTE-ROOM 2 KHAZANA · OPENING ONTO DIWAN COURT Y⁰ BELOW · MAIN HARIM MAJLIS 1
A' — A"
ROSHAN · ROSHAN · ROSHAN
D'

N.

MAIN SHOPPING STREET.

Labels in ground plan:
C' ADJACENT HOUSE 164 — C"
SHOP 1 · SHOP 2 · SHOP 3 · SHOP 4 · SHOP 5 · SHOP 6 · SHOP 7
UP. DISUSED STAIRWAY
LAT. · STORE
STORE
STONE CISTERN (UNDER)
UP
LAT.
STORE
B' — B"
PASSAGEWAY
UP TO HARIM
DIHLIS · UP · GUEST ROOM · DIWAN COURTYARD · UP · DIWAN PLATFORM
A' — A"
ROSHAN · ROSHAN
D"

GROUND-PLAN. (ENTRANCE)

1m 0 1 2 3 4 5 6 7 8 m

EARLIER AND LARGER TURKISH HOUSES

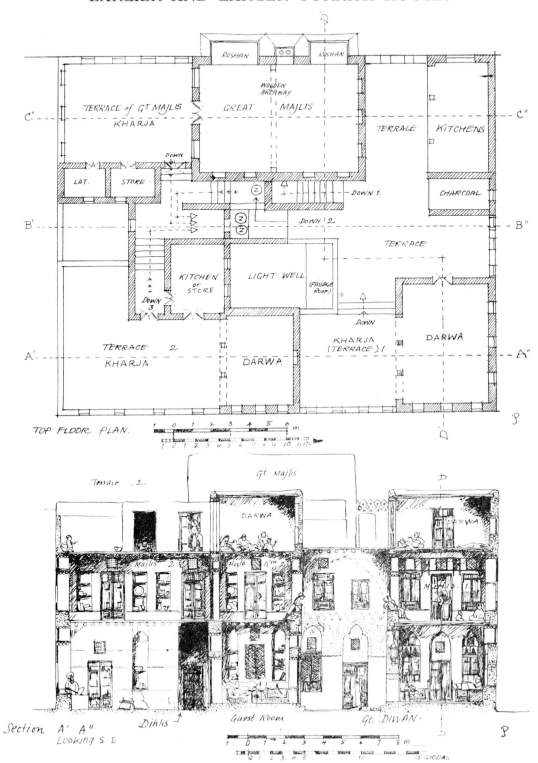

TOP FLOOR PLAN.

Section A'. A"
Looking S E

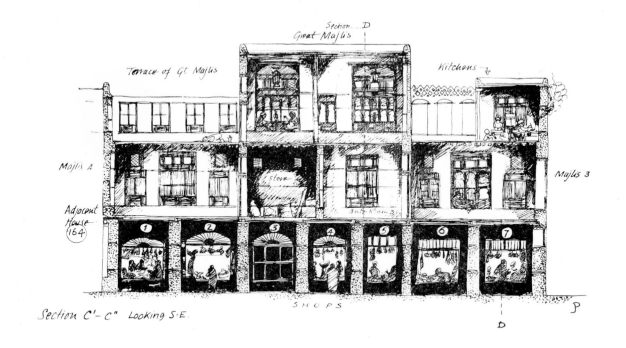

Section ... D
Great Majlis
Terrace of G.t Majlis
Kitchens
Majlis A
Store
Majlis 3
Adjacent House (164)
Ante Room 3
① ② ③ ④ ⑤ ⑥ ⑦
SHOPS
Section C'- C" Looking S.E.
D
P

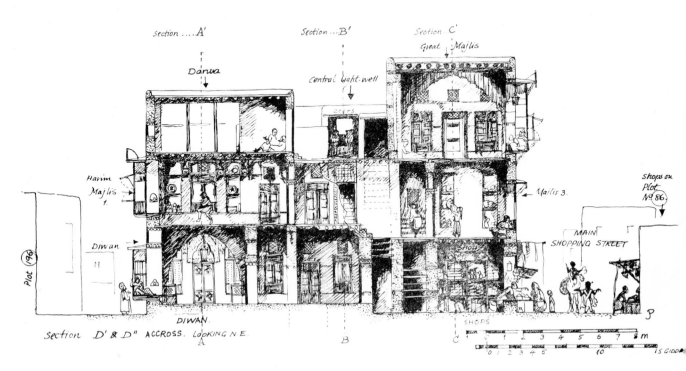

Section ..... A'
Section ... B'
Section C'
Great Majlis
Darwa
Central light-well
Shops on Plot No 86
Harim Majlis 1
Majlis 3
Diwan
MAIN SHOPPING STREET
Plot (96)
SHOP
DIWAN.
SHOPS
A
B
C
P
Section D' & D" ACCROSS. LOOKING N.E.

0 1 2 3 4 5 6 7 8 m
0 1 2 3 4 5   10   15 GIDDA

34

HARIM MAJLIS IN SHENNAWI'S HOUSE. No. 163

The House of the Sharifa Miryam on the Mainland.
(*No. 363*)

This house is unique and intact. It was built, like No. 65 on the island, for the especial needs of the Sharifa, widow of Sayed Osman Mohammed Taj el Sir and her servants or attendant ladies, but it is more spacious and comfortable. It shows how the Suakin style can be adapted to special uses. It is of uncertain date but I place it among the earlier buildings because of its size and unique features.

It is a long, thin, high building almost entirely orientated north-eastwards, facing the sea and the Island-Town. The cliff-like south wall is almost completely blank. A few ventilators and three windows alone pierce its otherwise featureless surface.

The ends too, one-room wide, are comparatively featureless. All the entrances and fenestration are on the north face. There is a narrow yard or *hosh* divided into two parts, of which one has a small watchman's room at the entrance. The ground-floor is high but almost entirely given over to storage. It acts as a podium, raising the rest of the building above the surrounding neighbourhood to provide an uninterrupted view of the sea. Access is through two doorways, each adorned with a decorated door-hood, the side one, in one yard,

for the ladies-in-waiting and the central one, which is very elaborate, two storeys high and hidden within a high entrance-porch or hall open on two sides. Two of the upstairs windows of the house also look into this tall, shaded lobby, from which the Sharifa may occasionally

ELEVATION of INSIDE WALL

36

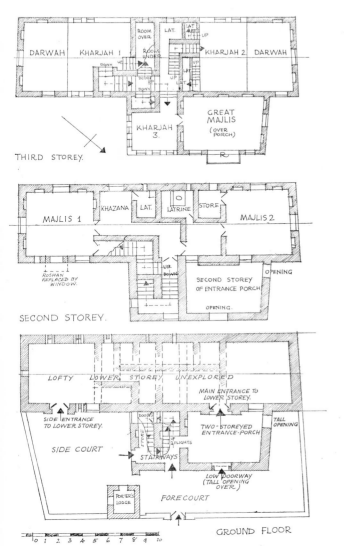

THIRD STOREY.

SECOND STOREY.

GROUND FLOOR

have shown herself to pilgrims assembled below. Apart from supporting the main *majlis* of the third storey, it is hard to understand any other purpose for this hall-feature.

Access to the upper floors is through two small doors into a dark, winding stairway which has a closing door half-way up. A small guard's room is at the top at first-floor level and access to the two wings is to left and right of it up steps and different levels.

The left-hand (east) wing consists of three rooms leading into each other, the first having a bathing-space and latrine attached, the second and third a store, also, but on the other side and partly under the stairway.

The right-hand main wing is of similar arrangement and the first two rooms have windows looking into the two-storeyed lobby already mentioned.

The third storey is the main floor. It is on split levels like the storey below. It consists of two wings and follows the arrangement of the rooms below. The two wings therefore together form two independent but inter-communicating buildings.

The main *majlis* however, is an additional room with a large *roshan* over the entrance-lobby below. It must have been one of the pleasantest rooms in Suakin when it was in use. The house is now uninhabited but it is carefully maintained by the Sharifa's family and is in a good state externally, having been substantially repaired in 1974.

This great *majlis* is entered through its own private *kharjah*. There are two further *kharjahs* on a fourth split-level, each with its *darwah*, store, latrine and bathing-space. The whole building forms a large somewhat lop-sided mass of buildings with some eighteen large and many other smaller rooms. It is thus one of the larger houses in Suakin.

CHAPTER SIX
THE SMALLER TURKISH HOUSES

Besides the large mansions described in the previous chapter, Suakin had dozens of smaller dwellings in the Turkish style, having *roshans*, decorated door-hoods, denticulated parapets and an almost standardised plan.

These houses varied in the number of rooms they had and were generally three storeys high. They were rarely found in isolation (they were too small and tall) but in blocks of two, three or as many as eight. The upper floors sometimes overlapped each-other and interconnected. It is convenient to begin with one typical house, No. 63.

1. House No. 63

This house occupied the corner of a block and would have had an adjacent neighbour. Two adjacent north and east walls each had *roshans*.

On the ground-floor there was: a *dihlis* and *diwan* with a raised sitting-portion on the left of the entrance-door, and on the right an extra store-room. At the back, left, the usual store-room, and right, the stairway with charcoal-store under the first flight and latrine half-way up.

On the first floor was the *harim* consisting of a *majlis* with *roshans* on the two external walls, and a store-room over the ground-floor store below. On the right, over the store, a withdrawing-room (*khazana*) with its own *roshan* and a separate entrance from the stairway behind. There were two latrines on the intermediate landings of the stairway, one above the other as mentioned in the description of stairway construction (p. 91). On the top floor, an enclosed terrace (*kharja*) with shuttered windows over the *majlis* below; and over the other two rooms a kitchen and a *darwa* or covered space.

On the island there were numerous examples of this basic plan with variations.

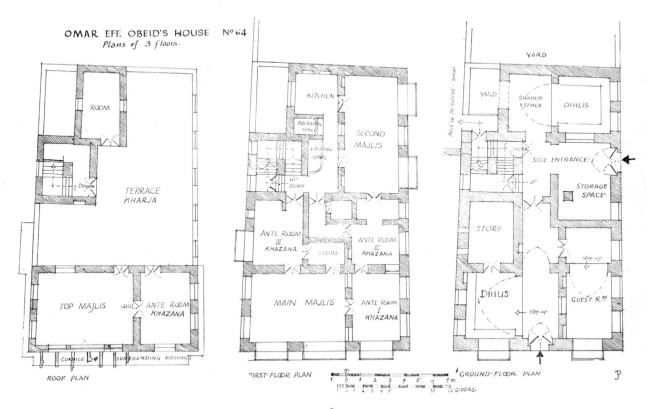

OMAR EFF. OBEID'S HOUSE Nº 64
Plans of 3 floors.

ROOF PLAN   FIRST-FLOOR PLAN   GROUND-FLOOR PLAN

38

THE SMALLER TURKISH HOUSES

OMAR EFF. OBEID'S NEW HOUSE Nº 64

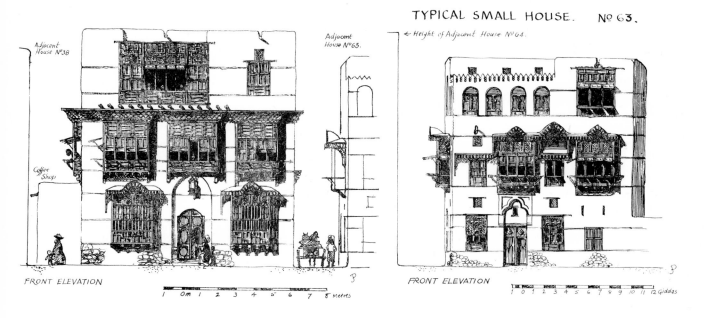

TYPICAL SMALL HOUSE.   Nº 63.

FRONT ELEVATION

FRONT ELEVATION

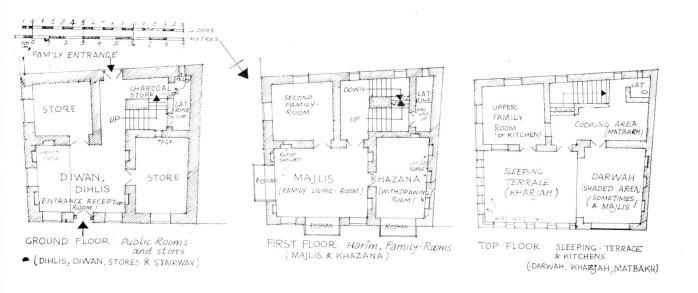

GROUND FLOOR: *Public Rooms and stores*
● (DIHLIS, DIWAN, STORES & STAIRWAY)

FIRST FLOOR *Harim, Family-Rooms*
(MAJLIS & KHAZANA)

TOP FLOOR   SLEEPING-TERRACE & KITCHENS
(DARWAH, KHARJAH, MATBAKH)

39

2. The House of Omar Effendi Obeid (No. 64) was a house of traditional design but of later construction, built in the 1880's just before the decline of Suakin. I describe it here to show its similar plan but different scale to the other houses.

In spite of its traditional plan and ornamentation, it had not the smaller scale and proportions of the earlier house No. 63. It was imposing rather than intimate. The two houses are illustrated together for comparison. It remained an excellent building however, and, with

its neighbours (one of which had completely disappeared, No. 38), made a pleasant street-front facing, unobstructed, the open sea until the National Bank of Egypt later planted its ugly, grey cement-faced Neo-Classic bulk right in front of them.

The ground floor had the usual *diwan*-store arrangement which we have seen in previous buildings (Nos. 163 and 63). The *diwan* half raised to form an *iwan*, was divided by the usual archway supporting the floor above. But it also had a large side-entrance and vestibule

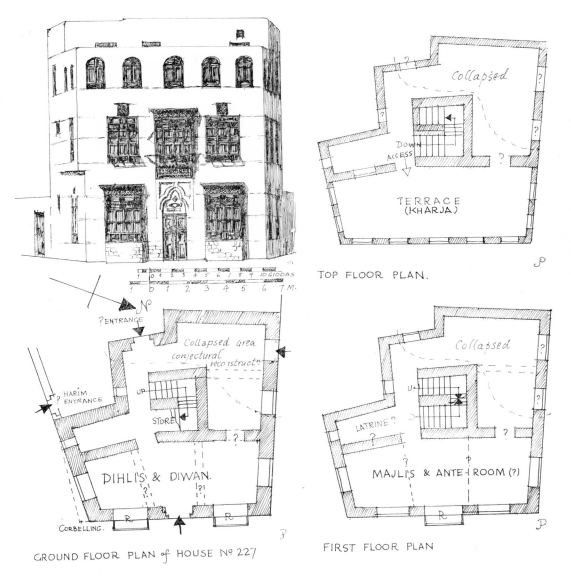

TOP FLOOR PLAN.

GROUND FLOOR PLAN of HOUSE No 227

FIRST FLOOR PLAN

next to which was a second, roomy *diwan* and court-yard, perhaps reserved for the attendants of visitors as in the house of Shennawi Bey (163). Through the courtyard, there was access to an adjoining coffee-house owned by Omar Effendi himself, which advertised itself with a painted notice, still visible in 1950:

RISTORANTE

E

CONOMICO

The first floor was taken up by two large *majalis*. The front one had three fine *roshans*, one of which had five instead of the more usual four bays; it also had two withdrawing-rooms (*khazanas*), one at each end. The second *majlis* and *khazana* were no-doubt for a second wife and gave access to an unusually large kitchen.

The top storey had a big *majlis-darwa* and *khazana* almost the whole north wall of which was taken up by a large, many-shuttered window. From here there was a fine view across the sea. Behind the *darwa* an extensive roof-terrace (*kharja*) with store and bathing-space was situated near the stairhead.

This house was particularly well provided with *roshans* of an elaborately ornamented "corniced" type. They were connected by a cornice-piece running continuously round two sides of the building. There were no less than eight *roshan*-spaces, but owing to the narrowness of the adjacent street, two of these were turned into large windows of *roshan*-size and design.

3. House No. 227

A single house of unusual design standing by itself on a corner site. The rooms were built around the central stairway and the plans are partly conjectural, the centre having collapsed at the time of writing.

4. The Other House of the Sharifa Miryam (No. 65)

This small, isolated three-storey house was not typical but it is worthy of mention because of its association with the widow of Sayed Mohammed Taj es Sir el Mirghani. (His large mosque and domed mausoleum are a feature of the mainland town). Its small dimensions are surprising by comparison with the more spacious house on the mainland described on p. 36. Perhaps it was only owned by the Sharifa and lived in by another member of the family. There was a small adjoining oratory or *zawia*, in the yard of which the pilgrims could assemble and pay their respects to the owner who could appear on the balcony at the back of the house.

The house was one-room wide, tall and narrow, with six large and heavy protruding *roshans*, two on each floor. It is surprising that it had not fallen down by 1950. It was divided into two parts, the main part at the front and domestic quarters at the back. It had three storeys in the front half and four lower ones at the back; this split-level arrangement was not uncommon in Suakin.

The front portion consisted of three, roomy super-imposed *majalis* each with two corniced *roshans*. The one and only door at the side, led to a *dihlis* from which access was had to the downstairs *majlis* or *diwan*. This was probably a waiting-room, for the Sharifa received visitors in a *majlis* upstairs. The third *majlis* above that would have been her own private quarters.

The rear portion of the building, which contained a staircase, formed an independent quarter for the rest of the family and servants. It consisted of a ground-floor storage-space with two, superimposed *majalis* facing north and the usual cooking-spaces, latrines and bathing-spaces. Halfway up, the stairs gave onto the balcony from which the Sharifa would show herself to pilgrims.

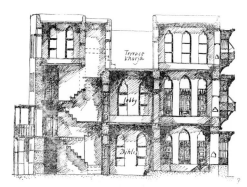

SECTION OF SHARIFA MIRYAM'S HOUSE No. 65

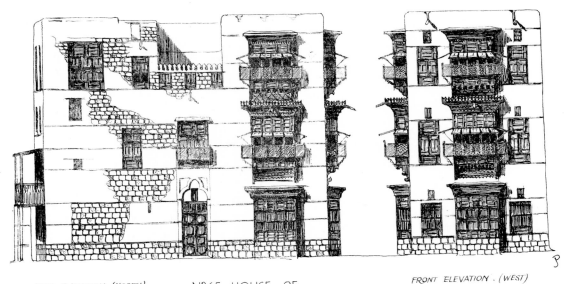

SIDE ELEVATION (NORTH)

No 65. HOUSE OF
ES SAYED MOHAMMED TAJ ES SIR
KNOWN AS SHERRIFA MIRIAM'S. HOUSE.

FRONT ELEVATION . (WEST)

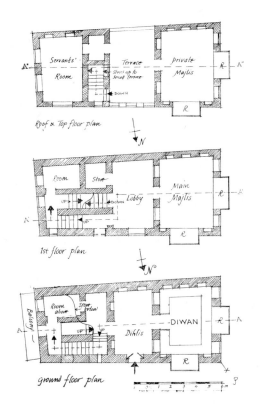

Roof & Top floor plan

1st floor plan

ground floor plan

THE GROUPING OF HOUSES IN BLOCKS

The houses so-far described were detached or semi-detached buildings occupying all or most of a site to themselves, but the majority of smaller houses, both in Jedda and Suakin were grouped in blocks or terraces of three and more. Sometimes the houses formed a haphazard conjunction, back-to-back or side-to-back. Sometimes they were built side-by-side to form a terrace and they were sometimes grouped with obvious intentional symmetry. (e.g. houses 169 and 172).

5. *The two houses occupying plot No. 59* show the plastic quality of a block as a whole. The houses were three and four storeys high respectively and their plans follow the usual arrangement. There are a few exceptional features such as the entrance-*diwan* of the bigger house, terraces at all floor-levels as well as on the roof, and a separate rear *diwan* in the smaller house.

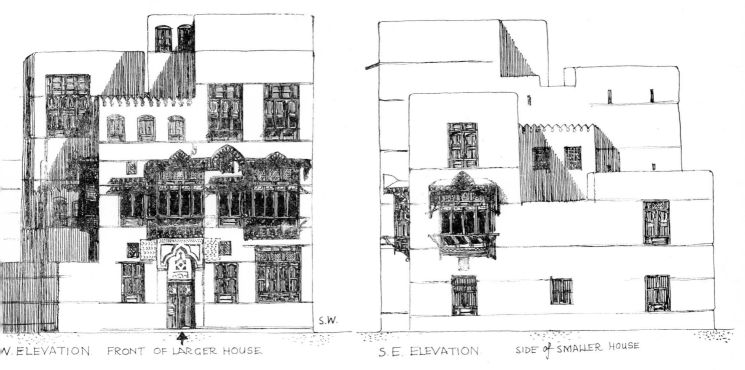

W. ELEVATION. FRONT OF LARGER HOUSE   S.W.

S.E. ELEVATION   SIDE of SMALLER HOUSE

A LARGE & A SMALLER HOUSE ON PLOT 59

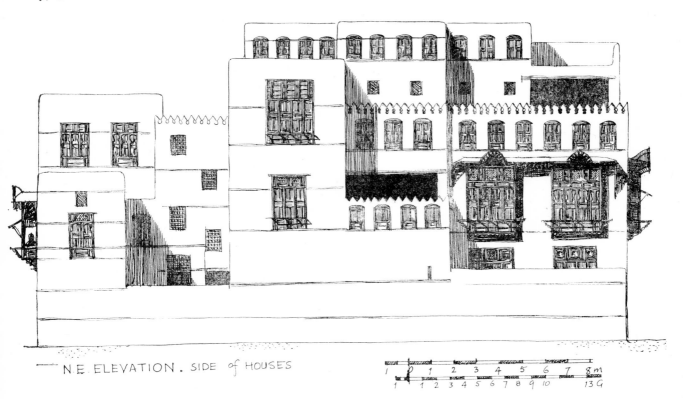

N.E. ELEVATION. SIDE of HOUSES

43

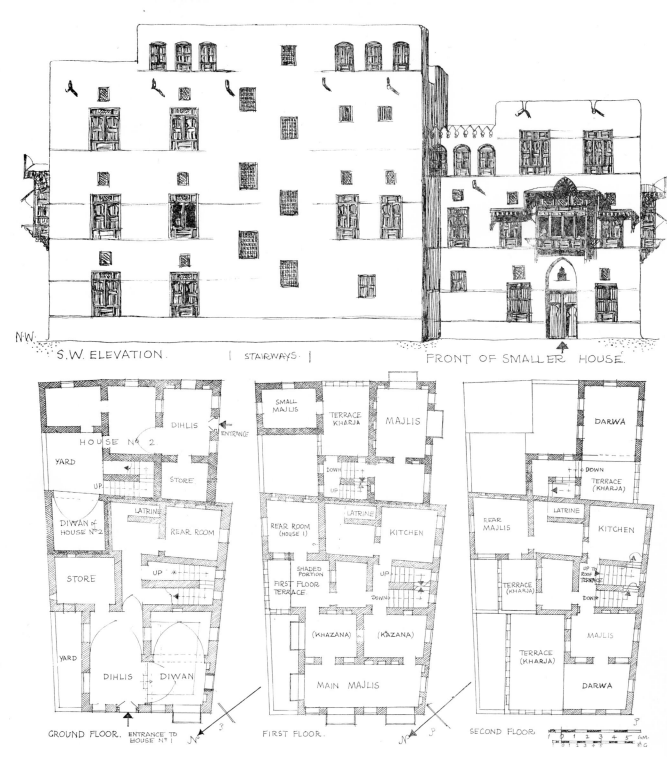

S.W. ELEVATION. | STAIRWAYS. | FRONT OF SMALLER HOUSE.

44

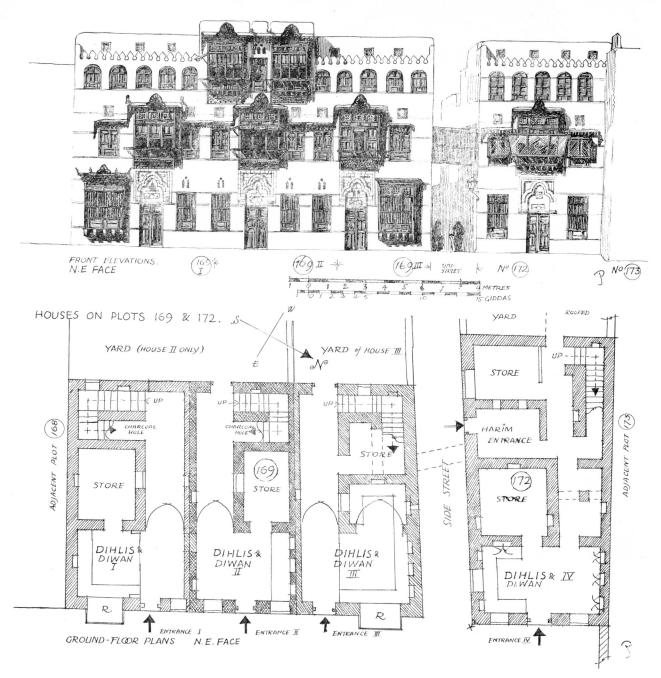

FRONT ELEVATIONS.
N.E FACE

HOUSES ON PLOTS 169 & 172.

GROUND-FLOOR PLANS   N.E. FACE

6. *The houses occupying plots Nos. 169 and 172* illustrate a terrace of houses. They were all built at the same time and the three occupying plot No. 169 form a symmetrical facade, dominated by a large central top-floor *majlis* with two *roshans*. A separate illustration shows the unusual *diwan* of the easternmost house. There was a bridge (*mamurr*) across the road connecting the blocks at first-floor level with plot 172.

The view from the roof-terraces of these four houses was especially interesting. They not only looked over to the usual blue seascape beyond the intervening buildings, but also faced onto the main square of the town in front of the Muhafaza where the main civic events took place.

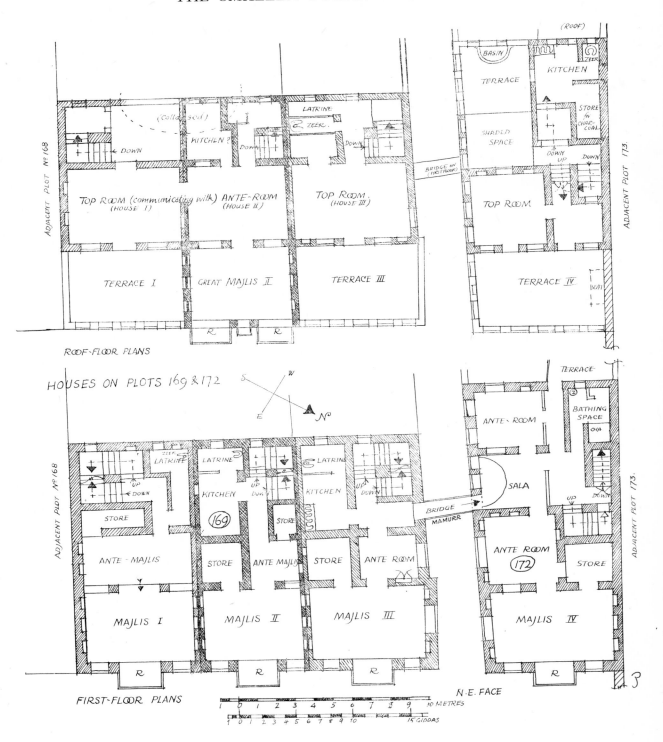

ROOF-FLOOR PLANS

HOUSES ON PLOTS 169 & 172

FIRST-FLOOR PLANS

N.E. FACE

EXTENDED VIEW of DIHLIS - DIWAN in HOUSE Nº 169 III

ENTRANCE DOOR

MAJLIS IN HOUSE Nº 169. I.

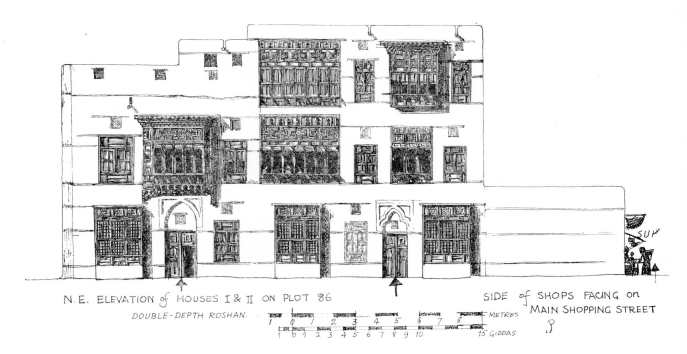

N.E. ELEVATION of HOUSES I & II ON PLOT 86

DOUBLE-DEPTH ROSHAN.

SIDE of SHOPS FACING on
MAIN SHOPPING STREET

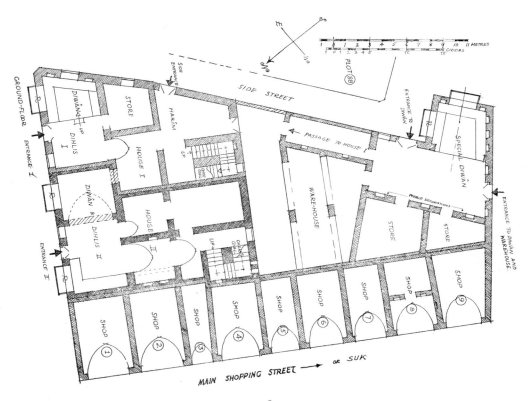

MAIN SHOPPING STREET → or SUK·

48

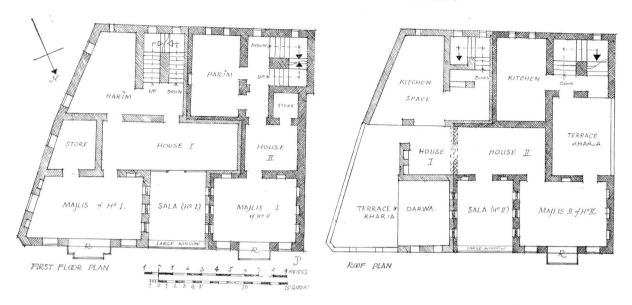

FIRST FLOOR PLAN

ROOF PLAN

7. *Two houses occupying plot 86* incorporated one or two unusual features. They were placed at opposite corners of one plot, the space between them was roofed-in and enclosed with large, wooden-panelled windows to form two superimposed loggias or *salas*. These two windows made the largest area of wood-panelling in Suakin, except for the window over the entrance-gate of the Wakala (p. 76). The remains of this panel were later made into a vertical screen at the head of the stair-case at the entrance to the Muhafaza.

The easternmost of the two houses had an exceptionally deep *roshan*, twice that of a usual one.

The western side of the block was occupied by a row of single-storey shops facing those on the ground-floor of Shennawi Bey's house (p. 29). Together they formed part of the shopping-quarter of the Island.

The back of the plot was occupied by a fine ground-floor *diwan* of later date with a large *roshan* looking up the narrow street. This *diwan* contained a small example of black-pebble wall decoration. The intervening space between this *diwan* and the main building was roofed-in to make a warehouse.

8. *Three houses on Plots 231, 232 and 233 "Beit Shams"* (p. 50).

This was the first large block of three to four-storey houses straight in front (east) on entering the island through Gordon's Gateway. It was approached from the hot south-west, featureless and least attractive side. On entering the little square to the left, the north-west front of Nos. 231 and 232 appeared with the unusual feature of a double tier of terraces on the third and fourth floors. The elevation is Turkish in style on the two lower floors, but the third and fourth were Egyptian, with round-topped windows, balconies and no *roshans*.

The elevation of house No. 233 was on the south-east end which, though a hot aspect, had a fine *roshan* and *majlis* and an Egyptian-style third floor with a large balcony. There was no fourth floor to this house.

A small two-storey Egyptian-style house was built over the corner of the plot. Access was from the far, north-east side with an external entrance on the first floor by a wooden stairway and balcony to the living-room. The room below had its own entrance, and may have been a warehouse.

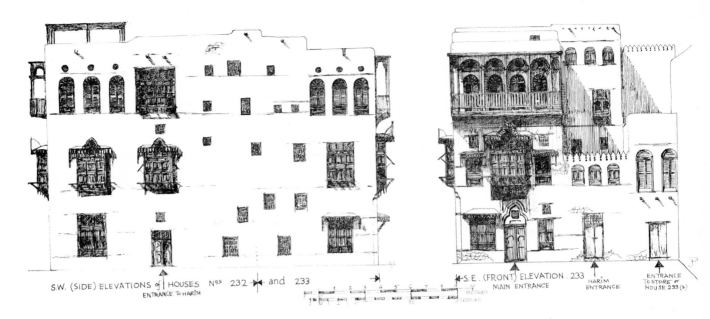

S.W. (SIDE) ELEVATIONS of HOUSES Nos. 232 and 233

ENTRANCE to HARÎM

S.E. (FRONT) ELEVATION 233
MAIN ENTRANCE

HARÎM ENTRANCE

ENTRANCE TO STORE of HOUSE 233(2)

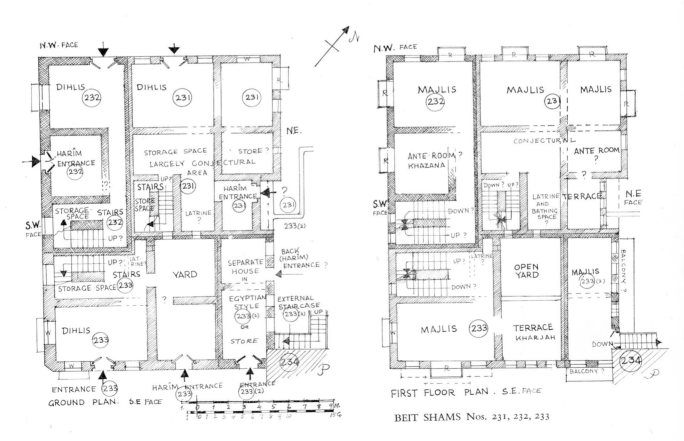

GROUND PLAN. S.E. FACE

FIRST FLOOR PLAN. S.E. FACE

BEIT SHAMS Nos. 231, 232, 233

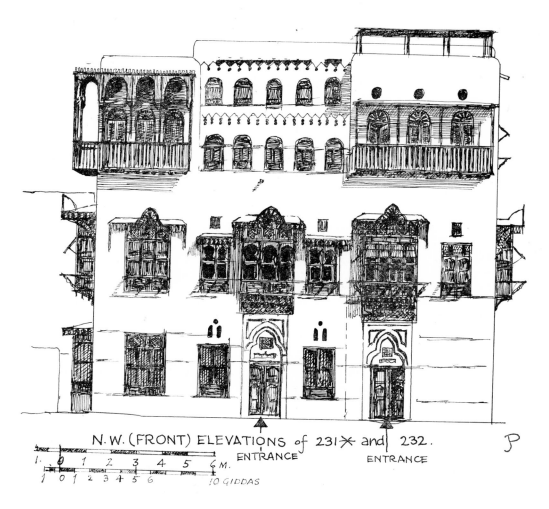

N.W. (FRONT) ELEVATIONS of 231✗ and 232.

ENTRANCE   ENTRANCE

1. 0 1 2 3 4 5 6 M.
1 0 1 2 3 4 5 6   10 GIDDAS

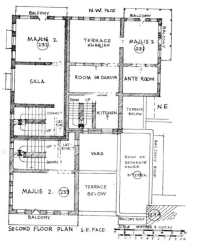

SECOND FLOOR PLAN S.E.FACE.

SCALE METRES & GIDDAS

BEIT SHAMS
Nos. 231, 232, 233

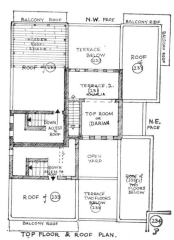

TOP FLOOR & ROOF PLAN.

51

S.E. ELEVATION of HOUSE 273

N.W. ELEVATION of "BEIT SIAM". 275.

N.E. STREET ELEVATIONS of HOUSES 273 & 274, & "BEIT SIAM." Nº 275.

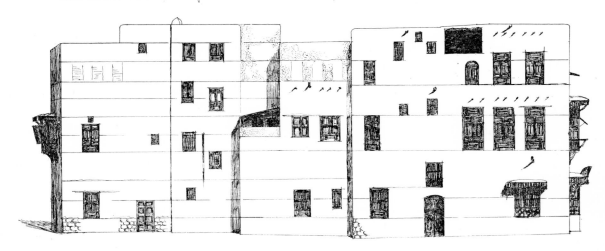

SOUTH (BACK) ELEVATION of BLOCKS 275 "BEIT SIAM" & Nº 273.

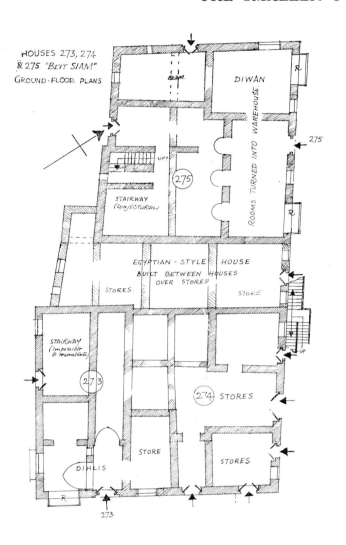

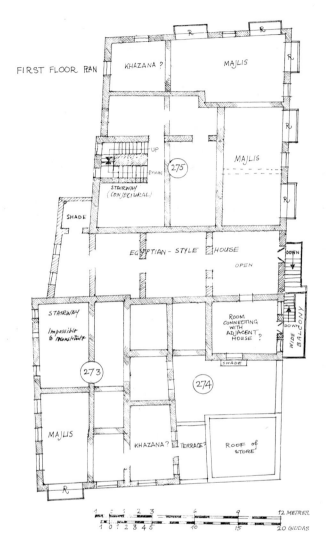

9. Beit Siam. (273, 274 and 275).

This large block near Gordon's Gate on the South of the Island consisted of two large, three-storey houses (273 and 275, Beit Siam) and two sides of the third plot 274, most of which was given over to stores. Another three-storey house in the Egyptian style was built later over the yard of 275 or what may have been a street at one time. A small single-roomed house was also built over one of the stores on plot 274. Access to these later houses was from the street by means of external wooden staircases leading straight onto wide balconies. There were similar houses and balconies reached by an external staircase on the plots opposite, Nos. 243 and 244. The street was the main thoroughfare to the Suk.

No. 273 had a fine ground-floor *roshan* with a deep overhanging *burneita*, and the first floor *roshans* of 275 Beit Siam proper, had large basket-type screens for privacy. It was in the little clearing before this house that the *Murjaiha*, merry-go-round, (p. 16) was erected during the 'Ids (public holy-days). It is shown leaning against the house-front in the elevation. The ground-floor rooms of this house had all been converted into warehouses.

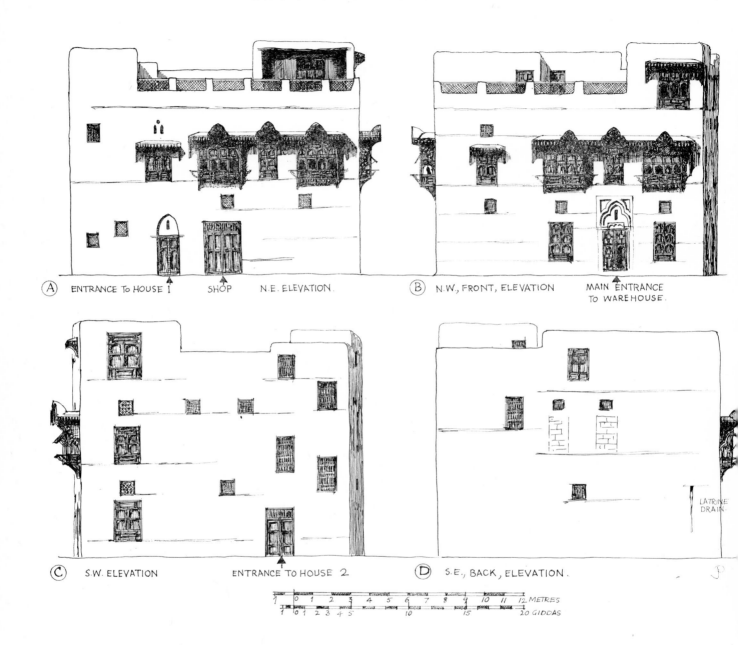

Ⓐ ENTRANCE TO HOUSE 1   SHOP   N.E. ELEVATION.

Ⓑ N.W., FRONT, ELEVATION   MAIN ENTRANCE TO WAREHOUSE.

Ⓒ S.W. ELEVATION   ENTRANCE TO HOUSE 2

Ⓓ S.E., BACK, ELEVATION.

LATRINE DRAIN.

1 0 1 2 4 5 6 7 8 9 10 11 12 METRES
1 0 1 2 3 4 5 10 15 20 GIDDAS

10. Two houses, shop and warehouse on Plot 93, owned by the Sharifa Miryam.

This consisted of two separate houses, a lock-up shop and a large independent *dihlis*, stores and warehouse on the ground-floor. Entrance to the two houses was at the sides, south-west and north-east, while access to the warehouse was from the front. The rooms were arranged about an open light-well above the ground-floor warehouse. Of the two houses, that on the north-east side had the better aspect and was rather bigger and better provided with *roshans* than the other.

54

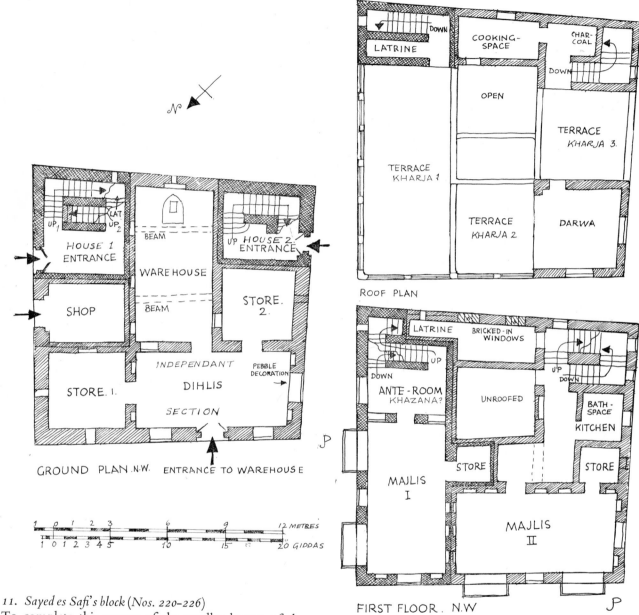

ROOF PLAN

GROUND PLAN . N.W.   ENTRANCE TO WAREHOUSE

FIRST FLOOR . N.W

11. Sayed es Safi's block (Nos. 220-226)

To complete this survey of the smaller houses of the island, eight houses occupying a large block are described.

The northern face of the block contained two house-fronts flanked by the side of another house and three lock-up shops (plots 220 and 221). The western side consisted of the three adjacent houses occupying plots

Nos. 221 and 222 to make a small terrace. The eastern street-front was more haphazard, with a block at each end and a small modern house halfway between the two. The southern side contained two three-storey Turkish-type houses.

BLOCK of EIGHT HOUSES ON PLOTS 220-226 CALLED "SAYED EL SAFI'S" HOUSE.

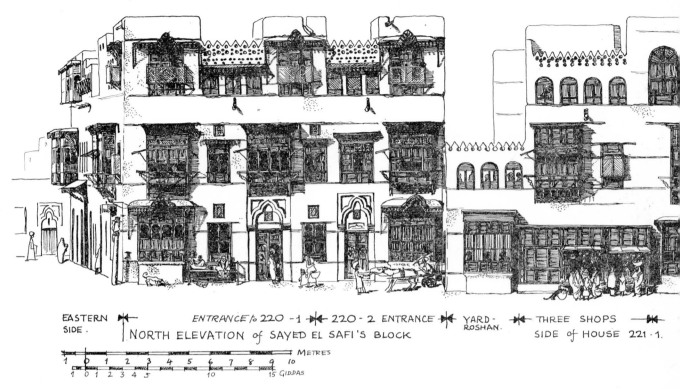

EASTERN SIDE. ⊢⊣ ENTRANCE to 220-1 ⊢⊣ 220-2 ENTRANCE ⊢⊣ YARD-ROSHAN. ⊢⊣ THREE SHOPS SIDE of HOUSE 221-1.

NORTH ELEVATION of SAYED EL SAFI'S BLOCK

1 0 1 2 3 4 5 6 7 8 9 10 METRES
1 0 1 2 3 4 5 10 15 GIDDAS

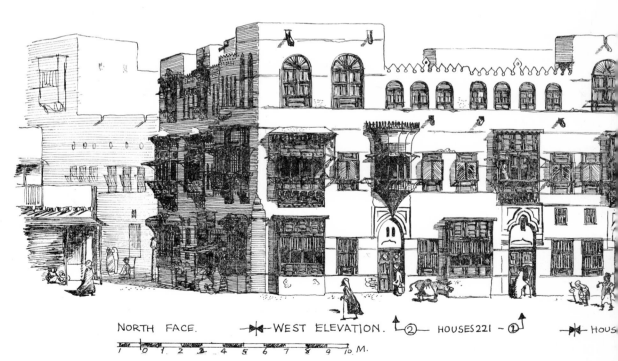

NORTH FACE. ⊢⊣ WEST ELEVATION. ②⌐ HOUSES 221 - ①⌐ ⊢⊣ HOUS

1 0 1 2 3 4 5 6 7 8 9 10 M.

The houses themselves require little comment. No. 220 had some interesting carved wooden cupboard-doors. No. 221 had wall-paintings in a room on the top floor; it had an unusual half-polygonal *roshan*. There was another such *roshan* in house No. 225, but I saw no others like them in Suakin.

No. 225 had the tomb of a holy man, Sheikh Farajallah, placed by its front doorstep. This is not uncommon in Islamic towns where great respect is paid to the dead. No. 224 was a more modest Egyptian-type house. It had no *roshans*. No. 226 seemed to be independent of the two downstair rooms which may have been stores or shops. It had deep first-floor *roshans* of an unusual design. The ground-floor *diwans* of many of the houses were turned into warehouses to deal with the sudden influx of trade after 1880. Their domestic character was thus often sacrificed. This is what must have happened here.

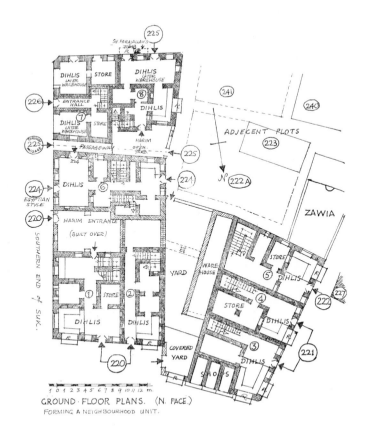

GROUND · FLOOR PLANS. (N. FACE.)
FORMING A NEIGHBOURHOOD UNIT.

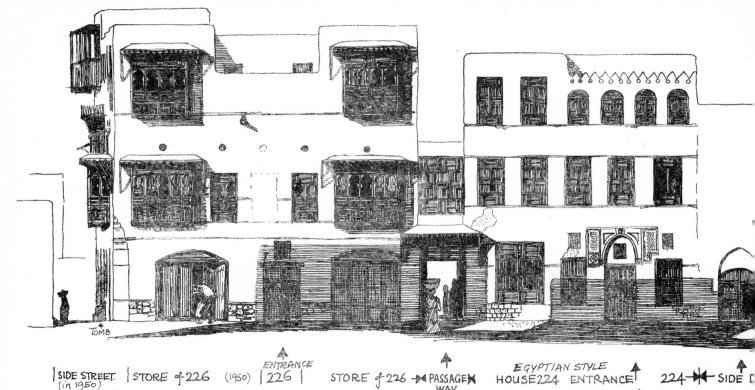

ENTRANCE

SIDE ELEVATION OF SAYED EL SAFI'S BLOCK (EAST ASPECT.)
AND SOUTHERN END of "SUK".

There were numerous other houses on the island which were interesting but to describe them all would be tedious. They often had interesting variations of detail but they generally repeat the principles which have already been illustrated.

To the east of the centre of the town was a group (Nos. 141 and 143) back-to-back, of which the easternmost was still inhabited in 1950 and in good repair. The other two houses faced westwards and presented four *roshans* on to the street.

Farther east again lay the house, No. 73, still occupied in 1950 by Omar effendi Obeid who also built No. 64, described above. He was living on there as late as 1950 with his family, vainly hoping for better times to return to Suakin. He once owned eleven houses whose annual upkeep was, he estimated, about £800. They were even then in ruins except the one in which he lived. Carpeted and furnished, the latter gave a good idea of what these houses in general must have looked like when lived in.

Returning to Gordon's Gateway and proceeding north by the main street, (widened and straightened by General Gordon), there was a large block (No. 2) of later buildings in the Arab style. They consisted of five houses and a number of warehouses. They were known as Beit Moh Ali Shawish.

For dignity, simplicity, economy and practical living, these little town-houses were hard to equal. I know of no more rational and sensibly designed, "standardised" houses anywhere else in the Middle-East. They did not have the picturesque, if quirky, quaintness of the medieval towns of Europe, and were nearer to the sophisticated refinement of the smaller Georgian town-houses of England. Yet they did not follow the strict symmetry and sometimes soulless geometric aspect of Baroque towns. They struck a happy medium between the two extremes of medieval quaintness on the one hand and geometric sophistication on the other.

On the practical level they were well adapted to make the best of one of the hottest parts of the world. Nothing more convenient and economical could have been devised short of air-conditioning.

The houses of Suakin made full use of local material resources without waste or destruction of the environment, were economical to build and maintain and there was nothing to go wrong, no plumbing or wiring. The fabric was an excellent insulator from extremes of temperature and would last indefinitely if properly maintained and the outer skin of plaster kept intact. The woodwork was solid and well-made, but also gay, almost playful with its fret-work exuberance. The houses achieved, without effort, the capacity to cater

220►◄ HOUSE 220 - 1.

HOUSES
►◄ 220 ►◄ SIDE DOOR TO ►◄ SHOPS & SIDE OF
1 & 2 YARD. 221-3.

comfortably for a varying number of people. To furnish them, all that was required was a number of carpets and rugs, a chest or two of crockery, lamps and cooking utensils; moving-in or out could be done in a matter of hours.

They were the products of the genius of a civilised society in the best sense of the word. They did not belong to a sophisticated and technologically complex civilisation such as those in the West today. They were the product of the sober, mature and unpretentious culture of Islam nearest its source, in Medina and Mecca, and still bearing the trace of its nomadic origins, with its imperative need to "travel light". An apocryphal saying of Jesus reported in Islam says "This life is a bridge, therefore pass over it, do not stay on it."

The houses of Suakin were beautiful because they expressed, very simply, all the complex qualities inherent in this culture and their disappearance is a great loss.

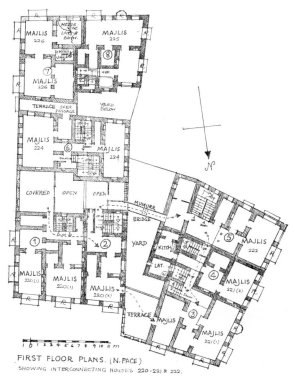

FIRST FLOOR PLANS. (N. FACE)
SHOWING INTERCONNECTING HOUSES 220-221 & 222.

SOUTH ELEVATION
OF SAYED EL
SAFI'S BLOCK
Nos. 225, 226

Tomb of Sheikh
Farajallah.

TOP FLOOR. PLANS . (N.FACE)

Signs of Decadence

The Turkish style in Suakin was showing unmistakable signs of impending decadence which had not however gone very far before European influences via Egypt began to replace the Turkish style altogether.

This may be seen in the increasing taste for over-elaborate and finicky decoration which was the fashion in both wood and stone-work. The *sharfa* fret-work decorations on the crests and bases of *roshans* at times verges on the absurd with the bird-like shapes of some crests, and some of the later doors, both external and internal, which were carved in tasteless, fluted roundels or solid wooden panels carved to imitate more intricate panelling.

It is evident also in the over-carved door-hoods of some of the later houses, notably those of Mohammed Bey Ahmed (No. 22) and the door-hood preserved in the courtyard of the Muhafaza.

Internally it is implicit in the rows of little finicky fret-work racks running round the *majalis* of the richer houses; notably Shennawi Bey's (No. 163 and 196) and in the houses of the Sharifa Miryam, Nos. 65 and 363 on the mainland where they were still to be seen in 1974. They are reminiscent of those which were common in British parlours of Victorian and Edwardian times, to house the innumerable bric-à-brac and souvenirs brought back from far places. They no doubt served a similar purpose for the merchants of Suakin. It seems that even the generous shelf storage-space provided by ten shelf-niches built into the walls of a room was inadequate to contain the number of ornaments collected. The final blow to the Turkish style was administered by the massive influx of trade on a twentieth century scale accompanied by the self-assured Anglo-Egyptian fashions. This led to the lower rooms of many houses being turned into warehouses; *roshans* replaced by store doors; inferior, Egyptian-style houses often of a mere two superimposed rooms, built over lower yard-space or added as a third storey to an already well-proportioned Turkish house (No. 233) and the rapid adoption of the new "style" by some of the leading families; the indiscriminate addition of the newly-invented oil paint (used, in Europe, to protect wood from the ravages of humidity and cold of its climate, but of little use by the Red Sea); the preference of balconies over *roshans*, etc., etc., and it is plain that the merchants and builders of Turkish-style houses had lost their belief in the excellence of their own traditions and were looking for something new at any price. This is the opposite of an age when people are aware of their own excellence and proud of it.

CHAPTER SEVEN
ZAWIAS AND MOSQUES

AMONGST the most interesting of Suakin's buildings are the mosques and *zawias*. They cannot of course be compared with the great mosques in Cairo, the Maghreb, Spain, Persia or Pakistan, but they do compare with some of the venerable mosques of Jedda which are of very early date. The mosques of Suakin are smaller, some of the *zawias* may even pass unobserved among the houses, the larger ones however, are built in the same traditional manner as earlier mosques and possess a simple dignity and the peaceful atmosphere appropriate to a House of Prayer.

Like most things Moslem, the mosque is a simple, dignified, straightforward affair with but few essential features.

It is not the habitation of a deity, sanctified by his Presence, but a place set aside for public prayer and for hearing the word of God in the Koran.

It is based on a domestic prototype — the Prophet Mohammed's own house in Medina — a courtyard surrounded by a verandah, probably not unlike the house of Khorshid Effendi in Suakin. It had a raised place whence the Prophet used to preach; this is preserved in the pulpit or *minbar* of the mosque with a flight of approaching steps from which, as a gesture of humility, the present-day preacher speaks, not from the top step but from the top but one.

All mosques are orientated towards Mecca. This is indicated by a small niche in the appropriate wall called the *mihrab* or *gibla* (literally "direction"). There should be entrances on three sides to facilitate access from all parts of the neighbourhood and the faithful are summoned to prayer by a *muezzin* who chants the call to prayer or *'azzan* five times a day, from a raised platform or a tower called the *maidana* or minaret. Within the courtyard or *sahn* there is a water-trough for ritual ablutions before prayer. Some of the mosques have a well for this purpose.

The faithful leave their shoes and step barefoot onto the mats or rugs in the prayer-area which covers the *mihrab* end of the mosque. This area is often extended as the congregation increases, first by a wooden shade and later by a permanent extension of another row of arches.

In the middle of the covered area there is a platform called a *kursi* reached by a short ladder, from which the Koran is read aloud.

This is all that a mosque requires.

ZAWIAS

A *zawia* (which literally means an "angle") requires even less. It is a private, local oratory used during the week, but not the Friday mosque or *Gaami* where all in the neighbourhood should go. It has no minaret since the faithful are not called to prayer; no *minbar* for there is no sermon, simply a *mihrab* to indicate the direction of Mecca.

A *zawia* is often attached to a house or group of buildings. The simplest form is little more than an enclosed area open to the sky, square or circular in shape, with a small apse-like protruberance to indicate the direction of Mecca. In the interior of the Red Sea country, it may be no more than a circle of stones picked from the ground in the desert hills. Such circles can be seen on the outskirts of a homestead, by railway-stations or out in the desert where some travellers have camped. In this improvised precinct the faithful say their prayers together. The enclosed platform illustrated on p. 63 is a small open-air *zawia* in Jedda.

The *zawias* of Suakin are mostly roofed-in, consisting of a single room, sometimes with a shaded extension outside or a low, walled-in area for praying out-of-doors. Three such *zawias* are illustrated on p. 63.

Musai and Magzoubi Zawias

The name *zawia* can, on occasions, be given to a quite imposing building; the Musai Zawia, on the mainland of Suakin, for instance, with its domed roof is said to have had three domes at some time in the past. If this is true, it calls to mind the little three-domed structure illustrated in da Castro's drawing (p. 9). The smaller of these oratories have obvious affinities with the plain, "original type" houses on the island, and the Musai Zawia has the same, buttressed wall-structure as Khorshid Effendi's house. (No. 35)

Another unusual and much revered *zawia* is that of the *Magzoubi* sect (p. 63). It is characterised by three large pointed arches on the north-east, *gibla* side.

OPEN PRAYING SPACE, JEDDAH

ZAWIA OF SIMPLEST TYPE Nº 110

QIBLA

SHADED PORTION

OPEN PRAYING SPACE

ZAWIA NEAR PLOT 68.

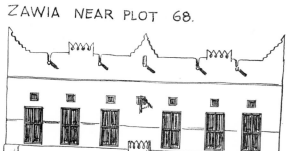

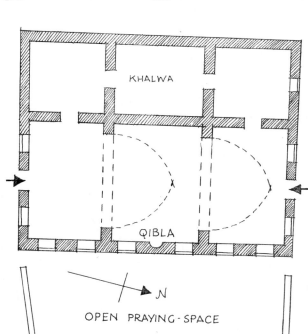

KHALWA

QIBLA

N

OPEN PRAYING-SPACE

MAGZOUBI ZAWIA

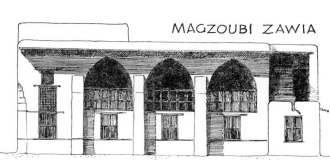

EASTERN FACE.

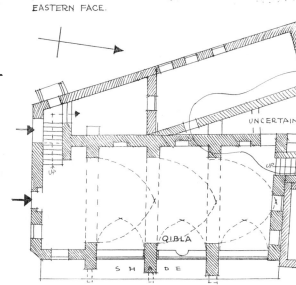

UNCERTAIN

UP

UP

QIBLA

SHADE

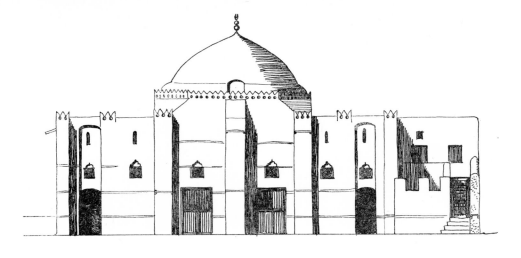

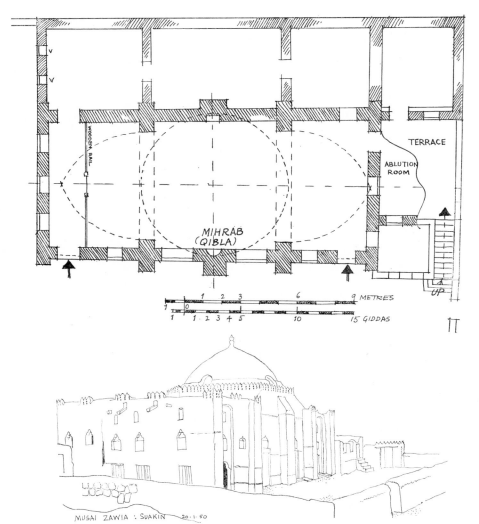

MIHRAB
(QIBLA)

WOODEN RAIL

TERRACE

ABLUTION
ROOM

UP

1 2 3   6   9 METRES
0
1 1 2 3 4 5   10   15 GIDDAS

MUSAI ZAWIA : SUAKIN   20.1.50

MUSAI
ZAWIA

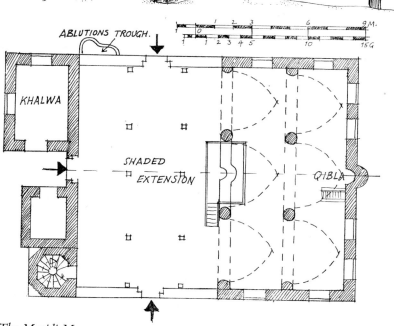

on pp. 22. Whatever its age, it is a simple and modest building in the spirit of *wahabi* Islam. It is, of course, still in use today.

Hanafi Mosque

Next to it in size is the Hanafi Mosque on the island, opposite the Muhafaza. It is less carefully built than the Magidi Mosque but on the same general scale. It appears in many views of the island because of its central position. It has some incised plaster decorations on the *mihrab* and a stone-built *minbar* (pp. 66-67).

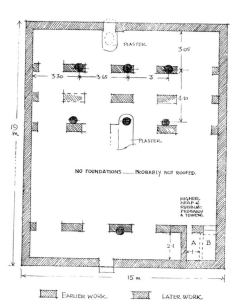

The Magidi Mosque

The oldest mosque in Suakin is reputedly the Magidi Mosque on the mainland. It is situated near the causeway leading to the island, next to the ruins of the large Wakala or caravanserai. The minaret has a carved stone parapet instead of the wooden rail of the other mosques. It is like many minarets in Jedda. The *minbar* or pulpit, too, is built of stone. Moreover it is almost identical in size and plan to the mosque on Iri already referred to

Above, plan of ruined 13th century mosque on island of El Rih of same dimensions as Magidi mosque.

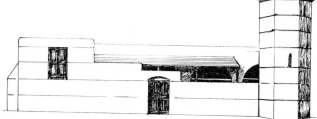

HANAFI MOSQUE. EAST ELEVATION.

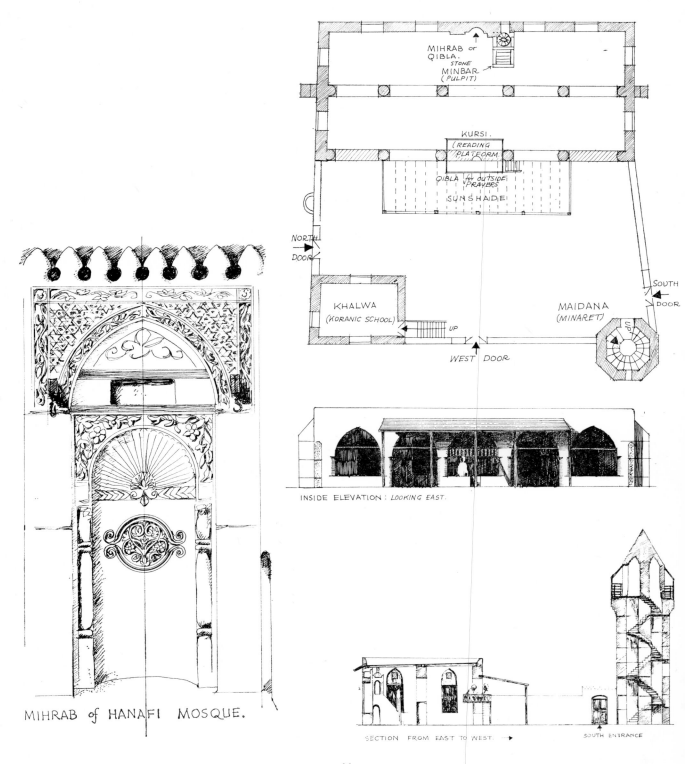

MIHRAB or QIBLA.
STONE
MINBAR
(PULPIT)

KURSI.
(READING
PLATFORM)

QIBLA for OUTSIDE
PRAYERS
SUNSHAIDE

NORTH
DOOR

KHALWA
(KORANIC SCHOOL)

MAIDANA
(MINARET)

SOUTH
DOOR

UP

UP

WEST DOOR

INSIDE ELEVATION: LOOKING EAST.

MIHRAB of HANAFI MOSQUE.

SECTION FROM EAST TO WEST.

SOUTH ENTRANCE

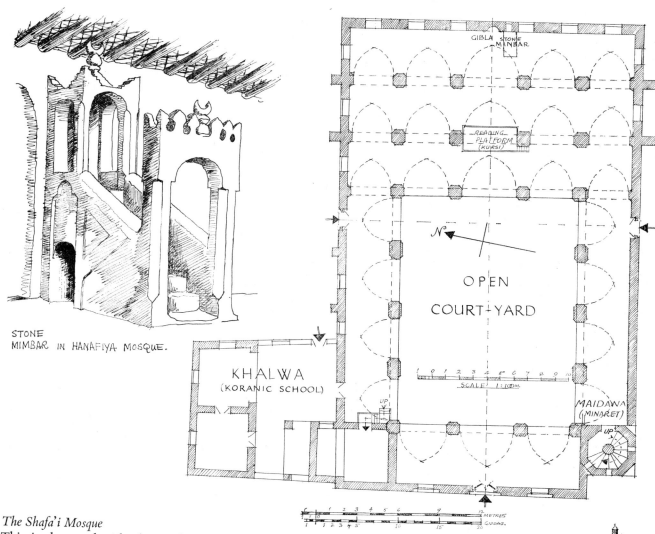

STONE
MIMBAR IN HANAFIYA MOSQUE.

The Shafa'i Mosque

This is also on the island. It is larger than the Hanafi
Mosque, more ornamented and of *sahn* type. Its entire
perimeter is shaded by a verandah of pointed arches.
It had a *khalwa* (Koranic school) attached to it. Its *mihrab*
and stone pulpit too, are decorated.

On the mainland, there are two large mosques whose
minarets pierce the skyline from afar. They are both of
recent date, being built at the end of the nineteenth
century; one by Shennawi Bey, after whom it is called,
and the other by the family and adherents of Sayed
Mohammed Osman Taj el Sir, whose photograph,
seated next to Mr Gladstone, was seen by the author in
the Muhafaza museum.

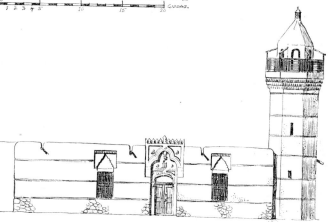

ZAWIAS AND MOSQUES

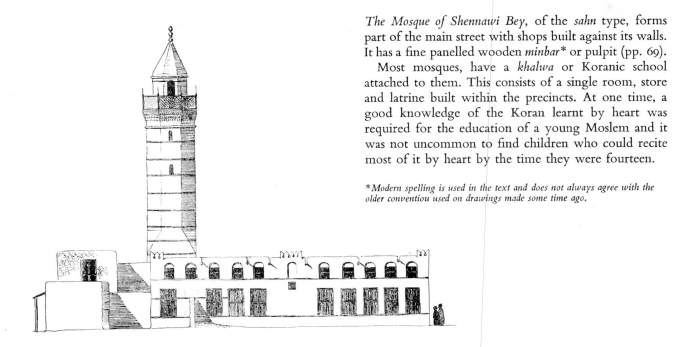

The Mosque of Shennawi Bey, of the *sahn* type, forms part of the main street with shops built against its walls. It has a fine panelled wooden *minbar** or pulpit (pp. 69).

Most mosques, have a *khalwa* or Koranic school attached to them. This consists of a single room, store and latrine built within the precincts. At one time, a good knowledge of the Koran learnt by heart was required for the education of a young Moslem and it was not uncommon to find children who could recite most of it by heart by the time they were fourteen.

**Modern spelling is used in the text and does not always agree with the older conventiou used on drawings made some time ago.*

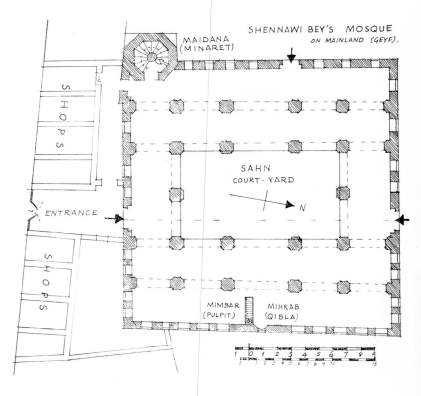

SHENNAWI BEY'S MOSQUE
ON MAINLAND (GEYF).

MAIDANA (MINARET)

SHOPS

ENTRANCE

SHOPS

SAHN
COURT·YARD

N

MIMBAR (PULPIT)

MIHRAB (QIBLA)

ZAWIAS AND MOSQUES

The Tomb or Gubba of Sheikh Abul Fatah is a truly beautiful little domed structure of pleasing proportions and ideal plan containing the tomb of the holy man and another person — possibly his wife? Its symmetry is best shown in the plan and drawing and needs no further comment.

PANELLED MIMBAR IN WOOD: MOSQUE of SHENNAWI BEY.

THE GUBBA of
SHEIKH ABUL FATAH
SUAKIN.

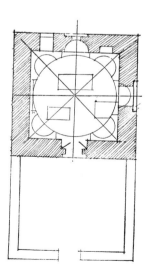

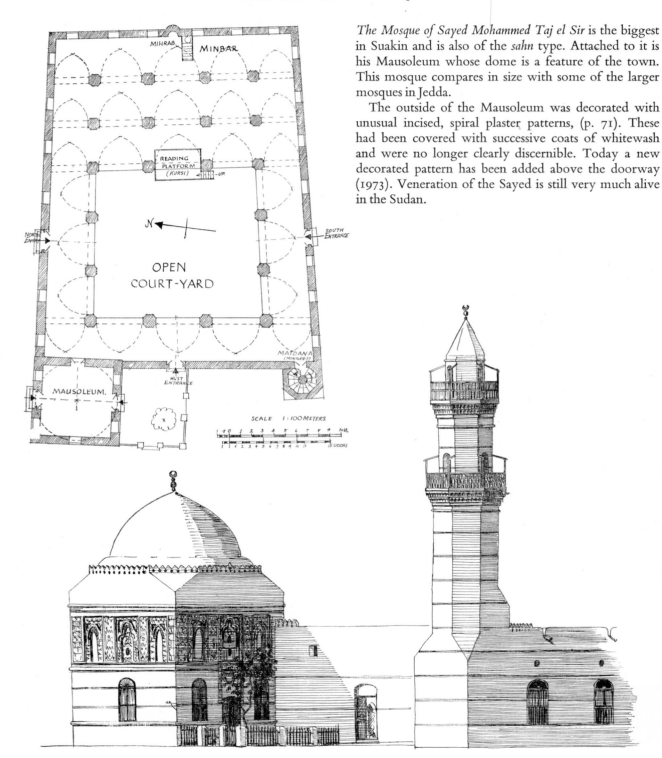

MIHRAB
MINBAR

READING
PLATFORM
(KURSI) UP.

N

NORTH
ENTRY

SOUTH
ENTRANCE

OPEN
COURT-YARD

MATDANA
(MINARET)

WEST
ENTRANCE

MAUSOLEUM.

SCALE 1:100 METERS

The Mosque of Sayed Mohammed Taj el Sir is the biggest in Suakin and is also of the *sahn* type. Attached to it is his Mausoleum whose dome is a feature of the town. This mosque compares in size with some of the larger mosques in Jedda.

The outside of the Mausoleum was decorated with unusual incised, spiral plaster patterns, (p. 71). These had been covered with successive coats of whitewash and were no longer clearly discernible. Today a new decorated pattern has been added above the doorway (1973). Veneration of the Sayed is still very much alive in the Sudan.

INCISED PLASTERWORK ON MAUSOLEUM OF SAYED MOH. TAJ EL SIR c.1946

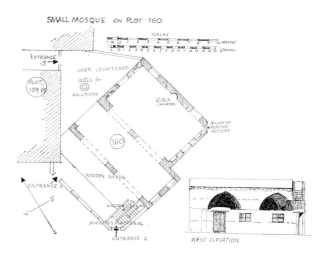

SMALL MOSQUE ON PLOT 160

SCALES

ENTRANCE 3

PLOT 159

OPEN COURTYARD

WELL for ABLUTIONS

QIBLA (MIHRAB)

DECORATED PLASTER PATTERN

160

WOODEN SHADE

ENTRANCE 1

MUEZZIN'S PLATFORM

ENTRANCE 2

WEST ELEVATION

Small Mosque on Plot 160
Sharply orientated towards Mecca, this little building with no minaret was more like a *zawia* than a mosque, but it was labelled as a mosque on the plan and had the necessary ajuncts for it to perform its functions as such namely three entrances, raised platform in lieu of a minaret for the *muezzin*, ablutions-well and though there was no *minbar* when it was surveyed, this is a movable part and may well have existed when it was in use.

71

CHAPTER EIGHT
EGYPTIAN STYLE BUILDINGS

LARGE BUILDINGS BUILT AFTER 1866
A few buildings form a transition between the older Arab-type of domestic houses and the later Egyptian type: *Three Gateways, The Muhafaza and Wakala*

Gordon's Gateway. The island was entered by the gateway erected by General Gordon when he built the Causeway in 1877. It made a very characteristic entrance-way to the island until it collapsed in about 1970. On either side was a guard-room and there was a wooden platform-bridge across the Gate. The Causeway could be covered by gunfire through the openings on the side. There were still two old mortars by this gate in 1974.

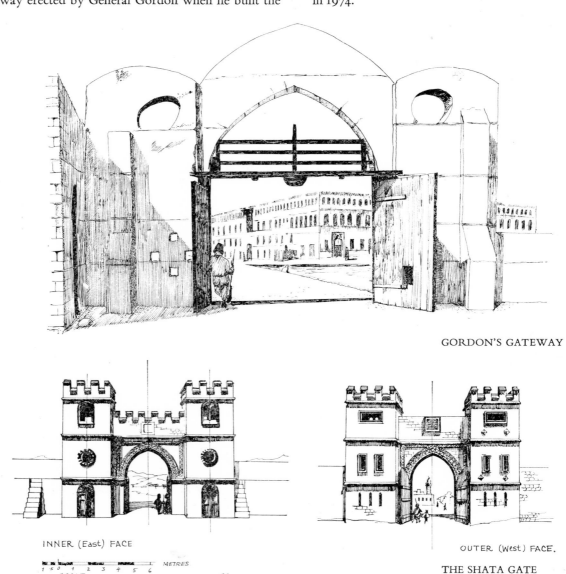

GORDON'S GATEWAY

INNER (East) FACE

1·50 1 2 3 4 5 6 METRES
SCALE.

75

OUTER (West) FACE.

THE SHATA GATE

72

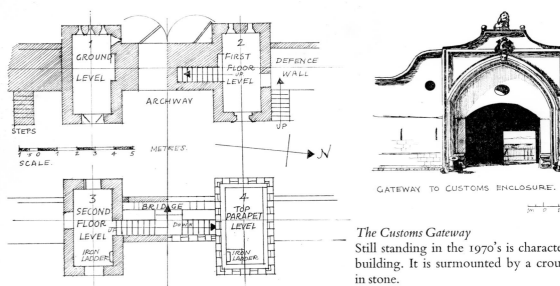

GATEWAY TO CUSTOMS ENCLOSURE.

The Customs Gateway

Still standing in the 1970's is characteristic of Egyptian building. It is surmounted by a crouching lion carved in stone.

The Shata Gate; Gateway to the Geyf or mainland town. This was also called Kitchener's Gate or Gate of the Eastern Sudan. It was more substantial than Gordon's Gate. Built by Colonel Kitchener in 1888, it was still standing and comparatively intact in 1974. It incorporates guard-rooms in its structure and was the only opening in the surrounding brick defence-wall, which he also built. This perimeter-wall is punctuated by a series of forts, some of which are quite large.

The Muhafaza was built by Mumtaz Pasha, in 1866 and a spacious residential second-storey with a wide verandah was built on the first floor.

One goes through a fine gateway into the entrance-courtyard which has a double curved ramp of steps sweeping up to the first floor of the building. Underneath them a door leads down to the water's edge and the built-over buildings beneath. At one time these

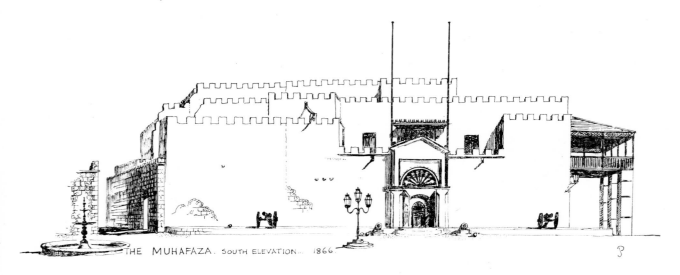

THE MUHAFAZA. SOUTH ELEVATION. 1866

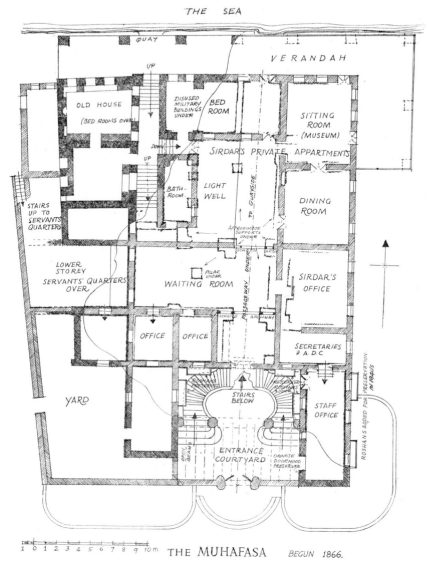

THE SEA

QUAY

VERANDAH

OLD HOUSE
(BED ROOMS OVER)

DISUSED MILITARY BUILDINGS UNDER

BED ROOM

SITTING ROOM (MUSEUM)

SIRDAR'S PRIVATE APPARTMENTS

BATH-ROOM

LIGHT WELL

DINING ROOM

STAIRS UP TO SERVANTS QUARTERS

APPROXIMATE SUPPORTS UNDER

LOWER STOREY SERVANTS' QUARTERS OVER

PILLAR UNDER

WAITING ROOM

PASSAGEWAY UNDER

SIRDAR'S OFFICE

OFFICE

OFFICE

SCREEN

ARCHWAY

SECRETARIES & A.D.C.

YARD

STAIRS BELOW

STAFF OFFICE

OPEN BEAM

ENTRANCE COURTYARD

ORNATE DOORHOOD PRESERVED

ROSHANS ADDED FOR PRESERVATION IN 1930'S

1 0 1 2 3 4 5 6 7 8 9 10m.   THE MUHAFASA   BEGUN 1866.

PLAN OF BOTH STOREYS:

might have housed military stores. At the top of the steps a large hall would have been used by those waiting to see the Governor whose office and private secretaries' offices open onto it. The large and comfortable living-rooms were shaded by a wide verandah facing the sea unobstructed on the north side and were grouped round a central light-well.

In the plan shown here, the top storey is correct in outline but the exact disposition and age of the foundations beneath is uncertain. The doubling of certain walls may have been necessary because of their age. The other buildings may be of any age prior to 1866.

Major E. O. Springfield, Commissioner of Port Sudan in the 1930's did much to save some of Suakin's buildings by forming a museum in one room of the Muhafaza and adding six *roshans* and a carved stone door-hood and various pieces of woodwork rescued from collapsing buildings. He also had a sum of £100 voted annually for the upkeep of the ruins.

ARCH - SCREEN IN MUHAFAZA IN EGYPTIAN-STYLE, TURNED, (KHARATI) SHISH.

Beit el Gedid or "The New House", built to contain the Government offices was an ungainly, four-storey building with verandahs and large windows facing the sea. It had little architectural merit but was an important building. I include it to contrast with the elegant and more modest buildings already described.

The upper verandah was later enclosed to form three rooms with two rounded windows each.

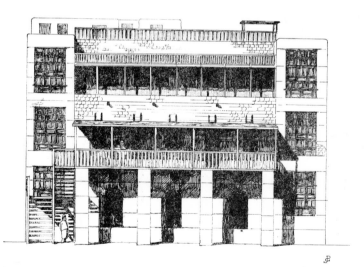

"BEIT EL GEDID" (THE NEW HOUSE). Nº 32.

75

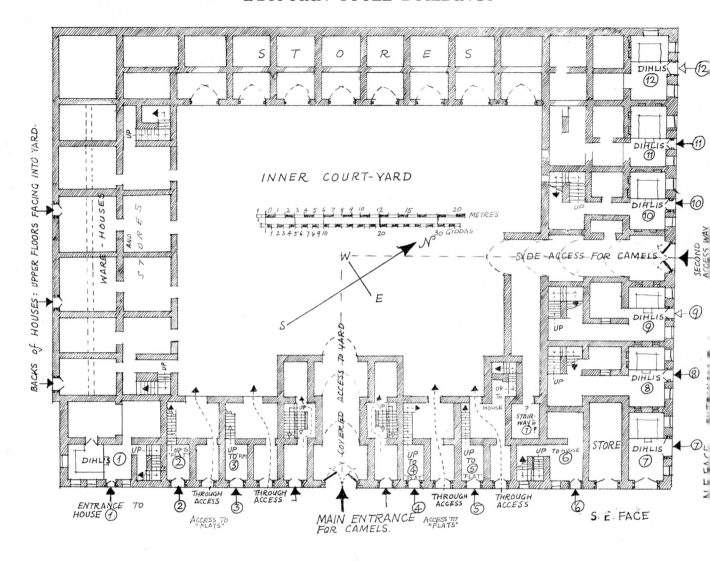

The Wakala or Caravanserai, completed 1881

This huge building was situated on the mainland by the Causeway, to replace the old *Nuzl* where the caravans of camels put down or took up their merchandise. It was a *khan* with independent quarters and houses for the merchants and storage-space for their merchandise in transit. It was the largest building in the town and probably the largest in the whole Sudan when it was built and was said to have been built entirely by slave labour. It was erected by Shennawi Bey, in anticipation of the boom which seemed to be coming to Suakin.

The Wakala was built on three floors with a roof-storey around a quadrangle some forty metres square within which a large caravan of up to one hundred camels could be loaded or unloaded. Entrance was obtained through two large doorways, one on the north and the other on the east wings of the building. The fourth, west side, was of one floor only and was taken up by stores and warehouses.

EGYPTIAN STYLE BUILDINGS

S.E. ELEVATION of WAKKALA.

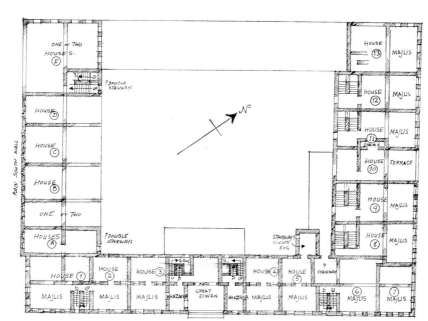

FIRST FLOOR PLAN. (SOUTH WING, PARTLY CONJECTURAL)

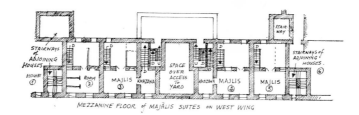

MEZZANINE FLOOR of MAJÂLIS SUITES on WEST WING

MAIN ENTRANCE GATE-WAY TO THE WAKKALA

THE GREAT MAJLIS OF THE WAKKALA.

The east side contained the main gateway in the centre with a large common-room over it having the largest shuttered window in the whole town. At each extremity of the wing there was a three-storey house and the space between them was taken up by smaller lock-up stores, flats or apartments. The north wing was composed of six adjacent and quite independent houses, three on either side of the second central gateway. The building is boldly conceived and well built and obviously no expense was spared in its execution. Both the stone- and wood-work are of the best workmanship and carefully finished off. The parapet denticules are intricately carved and number nearly two hundred. The south wing seems to have consisted of houses entered on the south but facing north on the upper floors, the lower floor, as usual, being given over to warehouses.

The Wakala was believed, like many large buildings, to have 365 rooms. This is a common cosmic exaggeration to do with the 365 days or "houses" in the astrologist's year. It was difficult in its dilapidated condition to count the number of rooms accurately, but there could hardly have been more than two hundred.

From the aesthetic point of view, the Wakala was more imposing than beautiful and it was quite out of scale with the buildings beside it, especially the revered little Magidi Mosque. Shennawi Bey's far-sighted enterprise was thwarted by the building of Port Sudan. The Wakala represented the considerable imagination of its sponsor, but it was hardly possible for him to foresee the revolutionary nature of Western influence with its railways, steamships and modern dockyards. The place was put to its true purpose for but ten years. After that, it housed Government officials for a time but it was too big and costly to keep in good repair and soon began to collapse. Its ruin is now virtually complete.

Private Houses built after 1890

The Turkish houses described in the previous chapters were built according to a tradition evolved and perfected in Arabia, especially in Mecca, Medina and Jedda, for the needs of rich cosmopolitan merchants, their families and a few retainers or slaves, most of whom lived with them. It was a comfortable, leisurely life in direct contrast to the arduous and dangerous trekking into the interior with the caravans or the hazardous sea-journeys around the Red Sea coasts. The *diwans* were the scenes of affable, if hard bargaining over cups of coffee during the day and the cool evenings were spent on the quays, in the streets or on the *kharjas*.

But the Nineteenth Century was to bring war and revolt to Suakin's very walls, and the restless Western World, seeking further afield for the sale of its merchandise, had cut the Suez Canal which was opened in 1879. This led to the settlement of rich, foreign trading-concerns like the Eastern Telegraph Company, the National Bank of Egypt, Gellatly Hankey, Mitchell Cotts and other private companies, not to mention the GHQ of the Anglo-Egyptian Army and enlarged customs and quarantine installations. Private houses were now required for the numerous clerks and other personnel of these establishments. All this meant a radical change in the style of buildings, for the new inhabitants, European and Egyptian clerks and merchants, required houses like those they had been used to in Egypt. For convenience I will call them Egyptian-type since they were built in a different way and to an entirely new plan derived from Egypt rather than Jedda.

The rapid purchase and development of all vacant sites to provide this accommodation, from 1890 onwards, was followed by a mushroom-growth of building by Egyptian masons using the local coral-like stone to achieve a smooth wall by dressing the madrepore into small square blocks on the outside and inside and filling-in with random rubble. Unprotected by the essential skin of plaster, these houses soon deteriorated and collapsed more quickly than their older Hedjazi-built neighbours. The two faces of the wall tended to fall apart for they were only held together by square *taglilat* which, unlike the round type of the

Turkish builders, did not "key" into each other (p. 90).

It was, unfortunately, by these newer houses that the buildings of Suakin as a whole were adversely judged. They were hurriedly built to a uniform plan with a monotonous repetition of identical semi-circular-topped windows and doors probably imported ready-made from Egypt. These items, European in origin, were much less suitable for the climate than *roshans*. The windows had louvred French-style shutters and the houses mostly had deep balconies which were sometimes wholly enclosed with plain criss-cross *shish* screens instead of *roshans*. These formed whole "rooms" projecting into the street.

The effect of these new features on the elevation was less satisfactory than those of the Turkish style. The repeated identical windows were large and competed in area with the plain wall-space. The balconies slashed the elevation into two or three horizontal strips, giving it a clumsy horizontal emphasis.

The larger size of the windows was suitable for air and light in Europe, but in the Red Sea climate this was not necessary or even desirable; *roshans* with their flexible system of shutters and lattice-work were eminently more suitable, controlling the flow of air, reducing light and excluding its glare.

When the defects of the Egyptian-style are accounted for, however, there is still much interest in these later buildings and a survey of the architecture of Suakin would be incomplete without mention of them.

In general, they follow the plan of Egyptian town-houses, many of which could be seen at Wadi-Halfa before it was flooded by the Nile. We may begin with the large, comfortable home of Mohammed Bey Ahmed who was Second-in-Command to Colonel Kitchener.

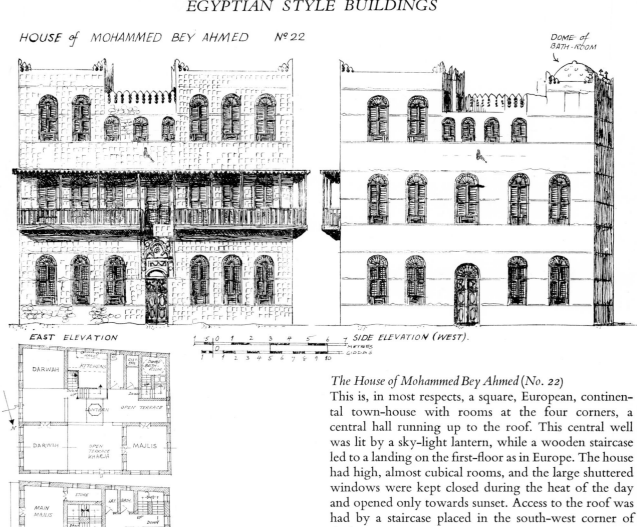

HOUSE of MOHAMMED BEY AHMED   Nº 22

DOME of BATH-ROOM

EAST ELEVATION

SIDE ELEVATION (WEST).

DARWAH · RANGE · KITCHENS · CIST ERN · DOMED BATH-ROOM
LANTERN · OPEN TERRACE
DARWAH · OPEN TERRACE KHARJA · MAJLIS

MAIN MAJLIS · STORE · LAT BATH
SKY-LIGHT above · STORE
MAJLIS (Painted Ceiling) · KHAZANA · MAJLIS
BALCONY

STORE · LAT
DIHLIS · CUPBOARD · STORE
EAST DOOR
DIWÂN · HALL · DIWÂN

NORTH FACE   FRONT DOOR

The House of Mohammed Bey Ahmed (No. 22)

This is, in most respects, a square, European, continental town-house with rooms at the four corners, a central hall running up to the roof. This central well was lit by a sky-light lantern, while a wooden staircase led to a landing on the first-floor as in Europe. The house had high, almost cubical rooms, and the large shuttered windows were kept closed during the heat of the day and opened only towards sunset. Access to the roof was had by a staircase placed in the south-west corner of the house.

Entrance was from the north and east sides. The elevations show what the house looked like, with horned corners and denticulated parapets effectively crowning it. The outer wall was covered with a coating of cement-plaster treated to imitate stonework but not tallying with real coral-blocks beneath it. The carved stone door-hoods (*'agd mawshah*) were among the most elaborate on the island. The round-topped lunettes above windows and doors had carved *shareikha* decoration and a deep balcony ran round two sides of the house on the north and east sides.

On the first floor, the main *majlis* had a rather crudely decorated ceiling painted with the newly-invented household paints which were then being imported and

used, rather sporadically, on the doors, windows and even *roshans* of some of the other houses.

An oriental feature was the little domed Turkish-bathroom, at the top of the house. There were the usual terraces (*kharjas*) on the roof and a large boarded-in kitchen-area (see above).

Shennawi Bey's New House (No. 196)

The Shennawi family were great builders. They not only built the house No. 163 already described, but the great caravanserai and the mosque on the *Geyf*, and also house No. 92. Shennawi Bey also built himself the great New House No. 196, described here and shown in the accompanying plan and illustrations. It was still occupied in 1950 and was therefore inaccessible, but with the photographs and the perimeter ground-plan on the Government survey map, the disposition of the rooms could be deduced. The *harim* was built above a spacious warehouse covering three-quarters of the plot

and entered separately through a wide door on the west side (p. 83).

The house itself had the usual separate entrances for *harim* and guest use. On the ground level was a lofty, detached external *diwan* 5 metres wide and 10 long, divided by a fine panelled arch-screen (p. 121). The doors and windows are amongst the best woodwork on the island and the *diwan* was most impressive.

No. 264 was a good example of a small, compact detached town-house in this later style. It had basket-like projecting screens round the upstairs windows which did not enhance the appearance of the building. Such windows, a kind of semi-*roshan*, are common in this later style of building (p. 84).

EGYPTIAN STYLE BUILDINGS

NEW HOUSE & WAREHOUSE OF
SHENNAWI BEY.
Nº 196.

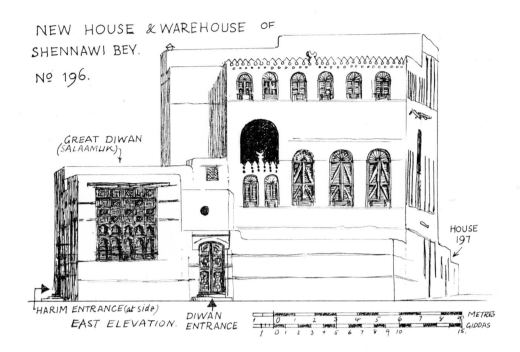

GREAT DIWAN
(SALAAMLIK)

HOUSE
197

HARIM ENTRANCE (at side)
EAST ELEVATION.

DIWAN
ENTRANCE

METRES
GIDDAS

GREAT DIWAN.
(SALAAMLIK)

197

NORTH-WEST ELEVATION. (SIDE)

WAREHOUSE ENTRANCE

82

SHOP AND DIWAN ON PLOT 197
with a variety of decorated niche-tops.

N.W. ELEVATION.

Other buildings in the Egyptian style
These small houses, like those of the Arab style, were often combined into larger blocks or terraces. The main street leading from the Causeway to the Muhafaza, which I have called "Gordon's Way", consisted of a long row of them.

Block No. 1 Beit Mohammed Bey Aboud on the left of the entrance gateway, was an example of eight such houses entirely enclosing a single old, Turkish-style house. Seen at a distance together with the great bulk of the Wakala on the mainland they gave the impression that Suakin was a modern European city.

No. 88 was a neat, low, two-storey house, still intact and in use in the 1950's which might serve as a model for future buildings if the island were to be repopulated.

SMALL EGYPTIAN STYLE   N° 88.

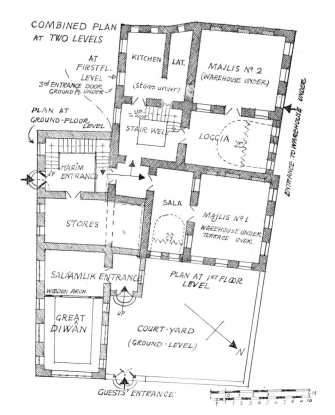

COMBINED PLAN AT TWO LEVELS

EAST ELEVATION. (FRONT).

HOUSE Nº 264.

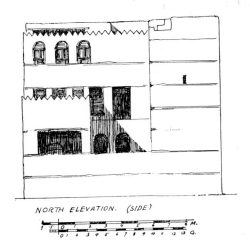

NORTH ELEVATION. (SIDE)

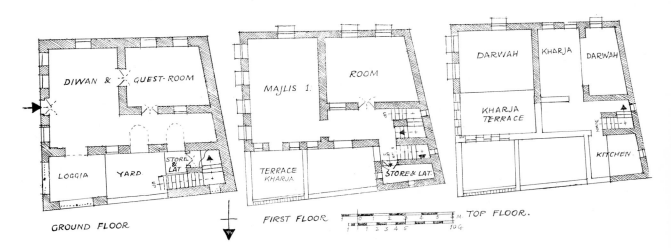

GROUND FLOOR

FIRST FLOOR

TOP FLOOR.

OTHER BUILDINGS

The National Bank of Egypt is the one building on the island which was completely out-of-keeping with everything around it. It was a large, pompous Neo-Classic affair, straight from Cairo or Europe, the outside of which was rendered in grey cement and it had little to commend it architecturally.

Between this and the Muhafaza was the large two-storey building of the *Eastern Telegraph Company* with verandahs and a balcony on the waterfront. It was later used as a rest-house and then pulled down.

The Mitchell Cotts building was also of a similar type and was still standing, though dilapidated, in 1970.

The Law Courts, opposite to Mohammed Bey Ahmed's house, was a single-storey group of offices disposed on either side of a central passage-way. One side was taken up by the large court-room with a raised platform at one end. It had a quite pleasing carved doorway of purely European style.

These buildings are mentioned because they can be seen in the various aerial and general views of the northern side of the island, and give some idea of the island's affluence at the turn of the century, but they are of little architectural interest.

CHAPTER NINE
MILITARY BUILDINGS

Fort Handoub, was a well-built pentagonal structure with high, battered walls of accurately cut coral blocks. Its unusual shape with barely a single right-angle is a great test of the masons' skill. Access was by a narrow draw-bridge spanning the deep surrounding ditch. The fort was protected by a perimeter wall raised high enough for the garrison to walk around the central tower without being seen from outside. It had a continuous raised platform enabling the men to use the wall to shoot across. There were two pentagonal redoubts at each of the western corners which contained six-pounder cannon.

The bottom compartment of the central tower was pierced by ten slit-shaped loop-holes placed high enough to shoot over the heads of those manning the walls. The upper floor which was supported by a central pillar of masonry was the guard-room and look-out post. It was attained by a retractable external ladder and surrounded by a solid wooden balcony deeply shaded from the sun. The roof was reached by an internal ladder from the guard-room and was used as a look-out post with a sentry shaded by a square sun-shade, as used by policemen on point-duty in Cairo.

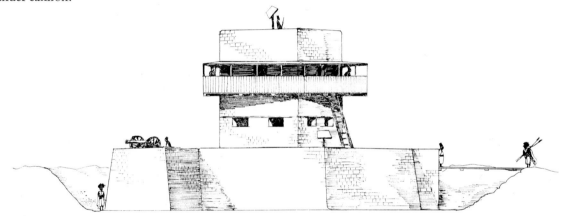

ELEVATION LOOKING NORTH.

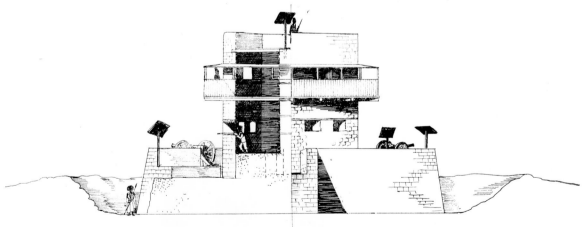

SECTION AND ELEVATION LOOKING WEST.

85

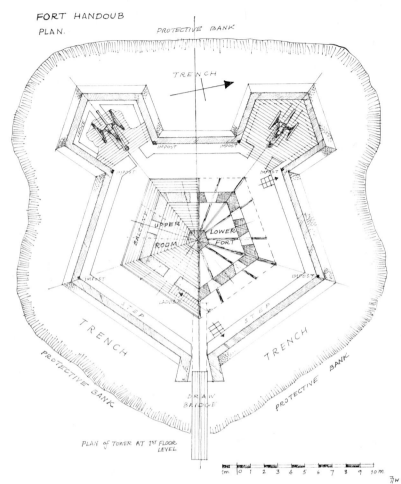

FORT HANDOUB
PLAN.

PLAN OF TOWER AT 1ST FLOOR LEVEL

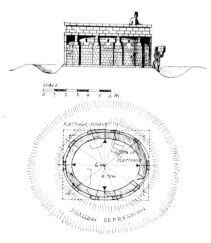

The Relay Post, half-way between the Fort and the town of Suakin was another well-built example of the Egyptian military mason's skill. It was a low, oval-shaped building with loop-holes and supporting buttresses, carrying a rectangular platform with a parapet reached by steps from within, which served as a roof on which the garrison could sit and stand when escaping from the dark cramped quarters below. *The GHQ* of later military Command was a large two-storeyed block of offices built round a narrow, rectangular courtyard. It was later bought by one of the local merchants and let out for a time, but was then pulled down to provide stone for the Suakin-Tokar road.

86

CHAPTER TEN
BUILDING METHODS

THE HOUSES and mosques of Suakin were built of madrepore, or rock-coral, brought from the sea-bed. This material varies a great deal in consistency and can be treacherous for building, especially if it is exposed to contrasting effects of the hot sun by day and damp, cold sea-air at night. Such alternation of temperature tends to make it crumble, so that it is essential to encase the walls in plaster. This uncertain nature of the masonry was counteracted by a judicious use of wood inserted in the walls and arches. This allowed for settling and contributed the tensile strength of wood and its elasticity.

The near-white plaster finish of the building had the slightly uneven surface which comes with hand-finish. It was the failure to maintain this protective skin that led to later houses collapsing so quickly. Originally the walls were not pure white but cream. They were, however, often white-washed over later.

The older buildings were built of large rough-cut blocks of coral or a porous conglomerate picked up from the ocean-shore where it was hardest. Stone was also quarried on the mainland. A little rough dressing with a large, double adze-shaped tool (shahuta) was sometimes necessary to remove protuberances but there was no attempt to cut them square to make a flush wall-face.

The blocks would, of course, be laid as straight as possible, and the thickness and regularity of the walls was kept constant by the insertion, at regular intervals, of horizontally-placed poles called taglilat. A sound understanding of their material enabled the masons to build a solid and abiding structure, given a minimum of maintenance.

The practice, introduced later, by stonemasons from Egypt, of squaring and dressing the blocks of coral picked up from the shore and already powdery and dry, as if they were stone, greatly reduced their size and strength. The Egyptian masons also left them permanently exposed to the elements, with no plaster-casing to protect them. Consequently the houses collapsed earlier than their far older neighbours and earned for Suakin the reputation of being shoddily built.

A lime-mortar made from the same material was used for plastering the walls and making arches. No scaffolding was used in building. The masons were supplied by labourers carrying the coral in palm-frond baskets (guffas) on their heads up inclined planks. As the work progressed a pulley was erected at the highest point and the material was hauled up in guffas. The work was done with a minimum of equipment. Some of the tools used are illustrated below.

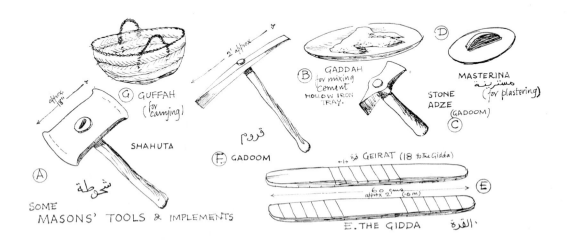

SOME MASONS' TOOLS & IMPLEMENTS

The first major course follows the plan of the house from foundations up to the level of the sills of windows and *roshans*, leaving gaps for the doorways. One or two courses of blocks were below ground-level to fill the foundation-trench up to the threshold-level which was usually one block above the ground. The first storey had external walls nearly 80 cm. thick, reduced by about 15 cm. on each storey; the second storey was about 66 cm. and the third 45 to 50 cm.

The second major course, at window-sill level, the position of *roshans* and windows was decided and, after laying the *taglilat* and keying cross-pieces, the building of the second course began. This brought the height of the walls up to the level of the lintel (*dashak*) of the doorways, halfway up the *roshans* and three-quarters of the way up the windows. At this level, the door-lintel was put into place and the recess left in the wall to accommodate the decorated stone door-hood or *'agd mawshah*. The lintel was usually decorated and often had a blessing in Arabic to welcome the visitor in the name of Allah. It also had two holes at each end about 19 cm. in diameter to receive the lugs of the door-shutters (cf. p. 113).

The top of the third course of masonry coincided with the lintel of the *roshans*, (the windows, three-quarters of the way up, had separate lintels over which a small ventilating hole or *taga* was inserted to bring the level up to that of the *roshans*) and brought the height of the structure to approximately 3.5 metres, or 6 *giddas*. The ceiling was another *gidda* above this, approximately half-way up the fourth course.

The fourth course of masonry was now begun.

The floor-beams were laid about 30-40 cm. apart soon after the lintels of the *roshans* and were let into half the thickness of the wall which was reduced in thickness on the inside by about 15 cm. making an appreciable difference in the size of the upper rooms.

Floors. The floor of the upper rooms was laid on these timbers. It consisted of a layer of thin canes or sticks 2-4 cm. thick laid diagonally across the beams, in threes and fours, and crossed by another layer laid across them, forming a diamond pattern between the beams. A layer of closely-woven palm-matting was laid over the sticks and covered with sandy earth on top of which a flooring-cement about 15 cm. thick was applied. This was, of course, again covered with mats or carpets for walking on. It was a heavy affair whose early subsidence deprived the walls of support and hastened their eventual collapse. Sometimes ropes were used instead of canes to support the floor between beams.

In the later, Egyptian-style houses, wooden boards were used for flooring but these lay uneasily on the irregular round wooden beams, and often had to be chocked up.

The fourth course of masonry was continued up to window-sill level of the first-floor windows and *roshans* which were considerably nearer the floor (50 cm.) than on the ground-floor. At this level too, the bases of the shelf-niches were marked; they were placed in threes on blank walls and in pairs on either side of *roshans*. There were sometimes seven in a room. This course was, sometimes, higher than the other courses to incorporate the thickness of the floor or to allow for higher *roshans* and ceilings downstairs.

The fifth course like the second, was half-way up the *roshans* and three-quarters of the way up the windows of the second storey. The windows had their own lintels inserted and, immediately over them, a ventilator-window as before. This brought the whole window and ventilator up to the level of the *roshan*-lintel and to the top of the *sixth course* of masonry.

The sixth course completed the second storey.

A seventh course, into which the roof or second floor was inserted like the floor into the fourth course, completed a two-storey building. Another storey might be added by building further courses in the same manner as before and reducing the wall-thickness yet again. In the case of a three-storey house, this seventh course, like the fourth, was also higher than the other courses. The second floor housed the main living-rooms where the *roshans* were often higher and wider.

BUILDING METHODS

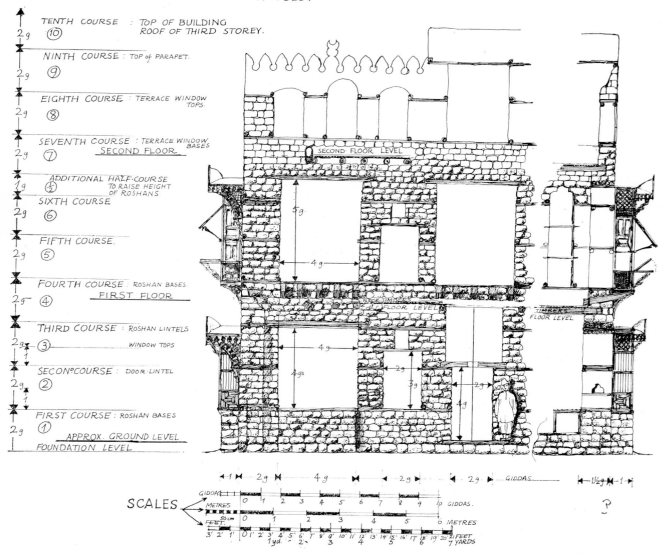

METHOD of BUILDING SUAKIN HOUSES.

TENTH COURSE : TOP OF BUILDING
ROOF OF THIRD STOREY.
2g ⑩

NINTH COURSE : TOP of PARAPET.
2g ⑨

EIGHTH COURSE : TERRACE WINDOW TOPS.
2g ⑧

SEVENTH COURSE : TERRACE WINDOW BASES
SECOND FLOOR
2g ⑦

ADDITIONAL HALF-COURSE TO RAISE HEIGHT OF ROSHANS.
1g ½
SIXTH COURSE
2g ⑥

FIFTH COURSE.
2g ⑤

FOURTH COURSE : ROSHAN BASES.
FIRST FLOOR
2g ④

THIRD COURSE : ROSHAN LINTELS
WINDOW TOPS
2g ③
1

SECOND COURSE : DOOR LINTEL
2g ②
1

FIRST COURSE : ROSHAN BASES
① APPROX. GROUND LEVEL
2g
FOUNDATION LEVEL

SCALES

GIDDAS
METRES
50 cm
FEET

The roof was constructed in the same way as the floors with a thicker layer of plaster-cement and sloped slightly outwards to drain off rainwater. Waterspouts consisting of hollowed-out palmwood would keep the water well away from the walls. Rain is rare in Suakin but when it does fall it is heavy.

Above this was a low parapet wall or a high wall with shuttered openings forming a ceilingless terrace-room called a *kharjah*. There was usually a shaded portion at one end which was called a *darwah*. The parapet was often crowned by denticulations (cf. p. 93).

Each floor thus consisted of three and a half courses of masonry, the fourth and seventh courses rather higher than the others. A three-storey building had some ten courses of two *giddas* each and a total height of 20/21 *giddas*, about 12 metres.

There were occasional variations. The masons were not rigidly bound by their rules and sometimes added a few *geirat* to the height of a course if it suited the requirements of their patron.

Masonry and Construction

The method of construction followed clearly-defined rules and standardised measurements, but they were not always rigidly adhered to. My observations were made during a brief visit to Jedda in 1951, and the time did not permit me to check them by comparisons between several houses. Enough is said here, I think to show the general principles and give an indication of the relative measurements and proportions used. A later investigator may be able to check my findings.

The measures used are *giddas*[17] and *geirat:* 18 *geirat* make a *gidda*, which is evidently the same as the Sudan *dura'* or "cubit". It is between 58 and 60 cm. or just under two feet (approximately an arm's length). and the dimensions of the houses fall naturally into complete integers of *giddas*. The masons use a *gidda*-measure as shown on p. 87 which is divided into three lengths of six *geirat* each; two lengths of six *geirat* at each end and one in the centre on the other side. This arrangement is ingenious and greatly facilitates measuring. A *geira* is 3.3 cm., or about one inch and a quarter.

The foundations of these houses were laid on the solid rock or flattened coral-face of the island; no other special foundations were needed. It was sufficient to clear away the surface-soil down to the rough face of the coral-rock and fill it in with one or two courses of masonry. The plan was decided by the size, position and orientation of the site.

The client and mason probably paced it out *in situ*, the only drawing being done on the ground itself. The size of rooms was limited by the length of available timber to span a room. Once it had been decided how big the house was to be, the position of the ground-floor *diwan* and entrance *dihlis* followed automatically. Next came the position of *roshans* and windows in relation to the points of the compass and to the neighbouring plots. Overlooking of the neighbours was avoided. This could usually be arranged by the judicious placing of windows.

The walls were built in major courses of 1.20 m. (2 *giddas*) high, held in place by the horizontal *taglilat* running along the top. Each major course consisted of about six courses of stone blocks about 20 cm. high. The *taglilat* were unplaned and round in section, in the earlier houses. They were made from a wood called *gandal* which was imported from India. They were held

in position by short pieces laid across them at intervals. Such short lengths of *gandal* were also used to turn the corners of the window and door-openings. They held the wall together. The weight of masonry in the courses above pressed and keyed them into the longer *taglilat*. Round timbers held the pieces together better than square ones would do for the roundness under pressure made dents in the circumference and so locked them together and prevented them slipping outwards.[18] (See below).

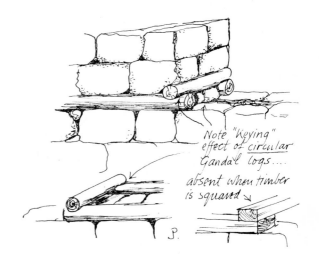

Note "keying" effect of circular Gandal logs.... absent when timber is squared

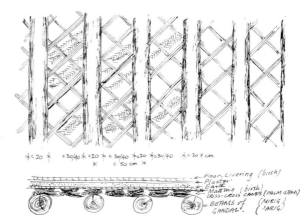

FLOOR & ROOF CONSTRUCTION

External and Internal plastering (Tangil)

The walls were plastered inside and out with a hard, plaster surface. The plaster, in some cases covered the wooden *taglilat*, but they were usually left exposed because they were useful for propping-up the wall when crumbling coral was being replaced in the course below.

The plaster adheres well to the rough surface of the coral but not so well if the coral is smoothed and cut down to a uniform size as in the later buildings. The plaster was often carved into ingenious designs which are described below.

Stairways

The stairways were constructed in a simple and ingenious manner. They were situated in the hot southern-most corner of the building where they also acted as a ventilating-shaft for the whole house.

The steps were arranged around a central rectangular column of masonry approximately 60 cm. (1 *gidda*) × 1.5 m. built in seven 1-*gidda* courses. They consisted of 1.5 metre lengths of small, unplaned, round *gandal* logs placed side by side and embedded at one end into the outside wall and at the other end into the central column. The wooden stairs were then covered with a layer of mortar to form a tread the fore-edge of which was kept in shape by a square wooden runner which could be replaced. The stairs rose in shallow flights of eight steps along the length of the shaft and three steps across the short side, (a rise of four), twenty being the average number of steps between each storey, making an average rise of 20 cm.

The stairways were well lit by large, strong grilles half-way up each floor and there were also little niches in the wall for lamps at night in the middle of each flight. On the intermediate landing there was usually a latrine serving both floors. The spaces under the first flight on the ground-floor and at the top of the stairway were used for charcoal-storage or added to the kitchen-space.

Arches, Corners, Corbelling and Parapets

The construction of arches was characteristically ingenious, combining the hardness of coral with the suppleness of wooden boards inserted between the voussoirs to take up any settlement in the arch. Wooden beams reinforced the corbelling which, being made of coral was of uncertain consistency and sheering-strength.

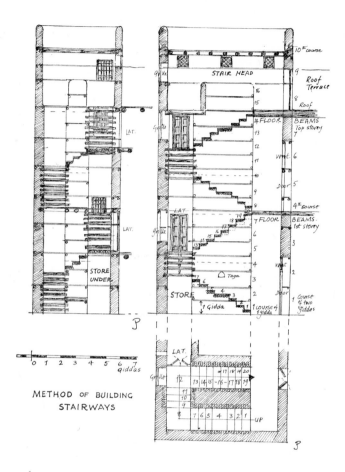

METHOD OF BUILDING STAIRWAYS

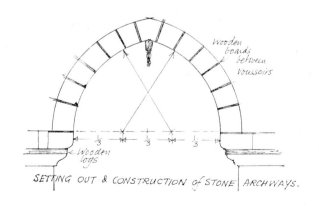

SETTING OUT & CONSTRUCTION OF STONE ARCHWAYS.

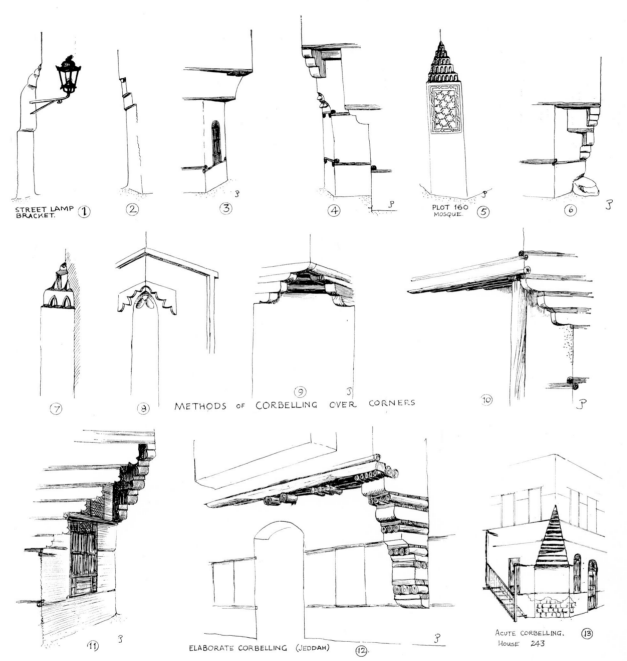

STREET LAMP BRACKET. ①

②

③

④

PLOT 160 MOSQUE. ⑤

⑥

⑦

⑧

METHODS OF CORBELLING OVER CORNERS

⑨

⑩

⑪

ELABORATE CORBELLING (JEDDAH) ⑫

ACUTE CORBELLING. ⑬
HOUSE 243

House-Corners

To facilitate circulation in the narrow streets and enable the horse-carts with their jutting axles to turn corners easily, the bottom-storeys of many houses were cut back and the upper-storey corbelled out in a variety of ways, sometimes with decorative additions to support the regular rectangular-shaped room above.

Street lamp-brackets were built into many corners for oil-lamps.

BUILDING METHODS

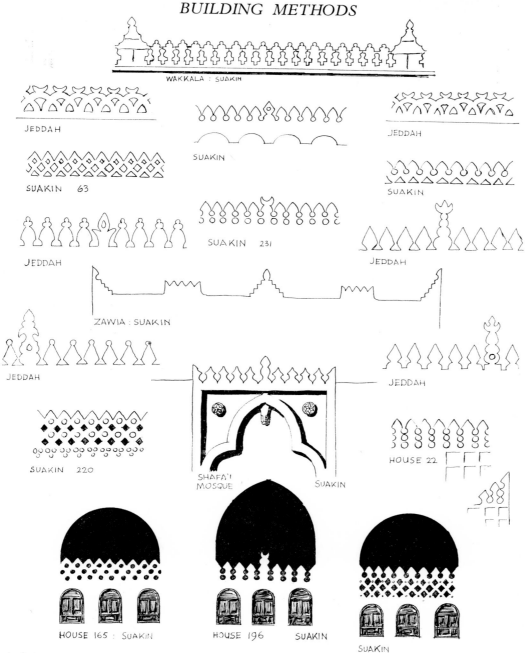

WAKKALA : SUAKIN

JEDDAH

SUAKIN

JEDDAH

SUAKIN 63

SUAKIN

JEDDAH

SUAKIN 231

JEDDAH

ZAWIA : SUAKIN

JEDDAH

JEDDAH

SUAKIN 220

SHAFA'I
MOSQUE   SUAKIN

HOUSE 22

HOUSE 165 : SUAKIN   HOUSE 196   SUAKIN

SUAKIN

Parapet Denticulations

The terraces were usually crowned with a denticulated parapet. This treatment was also found at other important points in the buildings, on the top corners, over the doorways and round the base of the domes of mosques. It was an effective way of finishing-off a building, and there were a number of different patterns.

It was less in evidence in the older houses and seems to have been a later embellishment. These parapets were built of carved coral blocks rounded at the top to drain off the rain and the whole covered with plaster. The denticulations were a simple but highly effective aesthetic device.

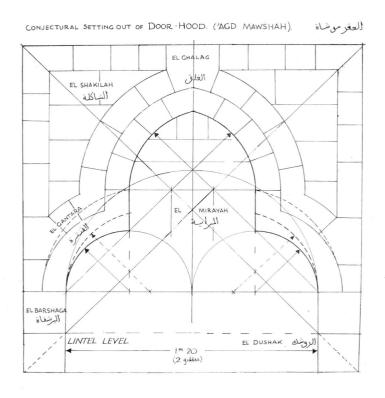

CONJECTURAL SETTING OUT OF DOOR·HOOD. ('AGD MAWSHAH). العقر موشاة

EL GHALAG
العالق

EL SHAKILAH
الشاكلة

EL QANTARA
القنترة

EL MIRAYAH
المراية

EL BARSHAGA
البرشاغة

LINTEL LEVEL

1ᵐ 20
(2 giddas)

EL DUSHAK الروشك

Nº 232.

Nº 184 BEIT EL BASHA

Nº 22 MOH. BEY AHMED.

STONE DOOR·HOODS ('AGD MAWSHAH.)

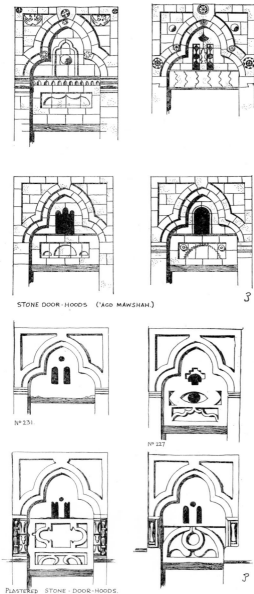

STONE DOOR·HOODS ('AGD MAWSHAH.)

Nº 231.

Nº 227.

PLASTERED STONE·DOOR·HOODS.

Carved Stone Door-Hoods ('Agd Mawshah)

True to the universal custom of decorating entrance-doorways, the builders of Suakin crowned their door-ways with a carved stone hood, called an 'agd mawshah. This was an independent, self-supporting section of sculpted masonry adding no strength to the structure of the wall into which it was embedded. The masonry

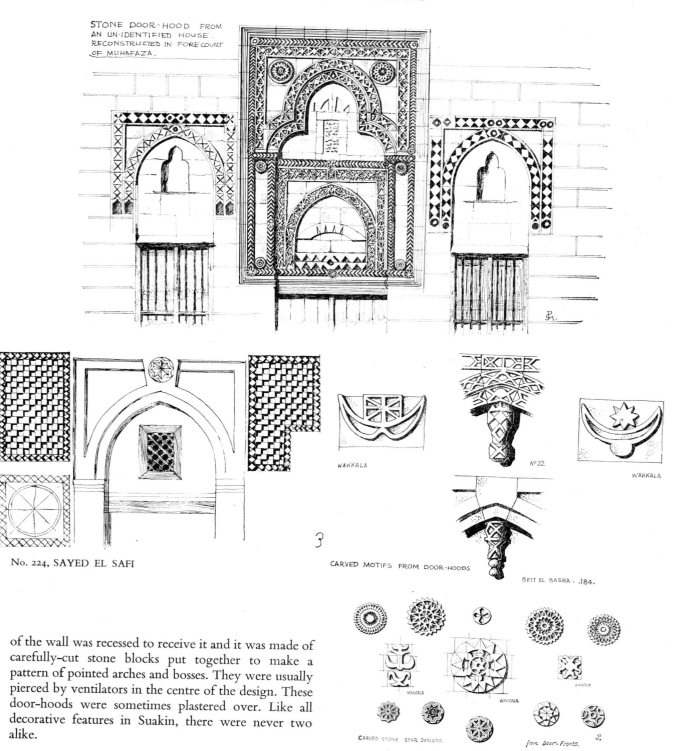

STONE DOOR-HOOD FROM AN UN-IDENTIFIED HOUSE. RECONSTRUCTED IN FORECOURT OF MUHAFAZA.

No. 224, SAYED EL SAFI

WAKKALA

Nº 22

WAKKALA

CARVED MOTIFS FROM DOOR-HOODS

BEIT EL BASHA . 184.

WAKKALA

WAKKALA

CARVED STONE STAR DESIGNS.

from Door-Fronts.

of the wall was recessed to receive it and it was made of carefully-cut stone blocks put together to make a pattern of pointed arches and bosses. They were usually pierced by ventilators in the centre of the design. These door-hoods were sometimes plastered over. Like all decorative features in Suakin, there were never two alike.

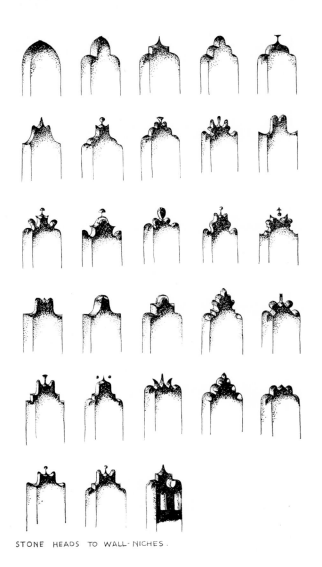

STONE HEADS TO WALL-NICHES.

Carved Stone and Plaster Decorations were carved on mosques and other buildings, usually in the *mihrab*, *minbar* and above the doorways. Mosque-furniture was often made of carved stone (pp. 66-67).

Incised Plaster and Pebble Decorations (Tangil)
The walls of many of the houses were decorated both inside and out with geometric patterns incised in the plaster. Small black pebbles were sometimes inserted. The latter were usually reserved for the interior of the

diwan and exterior of the richer houses. Both the interior and exterior of a mosque might be decorated in this way, especially the doorways and principle parts like the *minbar* and *mihrab*.

In Suakin, the outsides of the buildings were seldom treated in this manner, but in Jedda the walls of many houses are entirely covered with such patterns. They were found in one or two houses in Suakin, especially the *diwans* of Khorshid Effendi and Shennawi Bey's houses, House No. 173 and some of the mosques.
A few of the main designs are illustrated here. They are (1) the traditional, goemetric patterns usually found in Islamic art and (2) floral designs with symbolic elements. Their incorporation into a larger scheme with borders, pebbles and even floral elements was often most complex.

Method of making the Patterns
The walls of the room were first divided into rectangular panels between or above the windows, niches and door-ways, separated horizontally by double bands. Each area was then filled with an "all-over" geometric or floral pattern. Lunettes above arched windows and doors and the under-edge of archways were also decorated. This piecemeal working was necessary as a panel had to be completed while the plaster was still damp.

The geometric designs were square or hexagonal and cut on a simple square or equilateral-triangular grid which was first lightly scratched on the surface of the plaster. The pattern was then deeply etched right down to the yellowish stone underneath, giving it a pleasant contrasting background which was unfortunately lost when the wall was whitewashed over.

A considerable variety of patterns is possible on this grid principle. In hexagonal designs the main "units" of pattern are the triangle, hexagon, six-pointed "Star of David' or hexagram. (Squares or right-angle triangles on the rectangular grids.) These units are separated by secondary linear elements in the intervening spaces, consisting of single, double or treble lines, "V" shapes, "L", "Z" shapes, triskele and other patterns of considerable ingenuity.

Floral designs consisted of bands of wavy lines with alternating leaves or flowers, or panels with a "Tree of Life" motif issuing from a pot. This motif is still common in the Middle East, and is of very old Mediterranean origin.

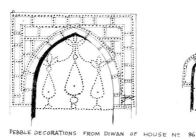

PEBBLE DECORATIONS FROM DIWAN OF HOUSE Nº 86.

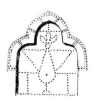

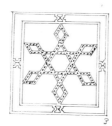

STONE CARVED BAND MOTIFS.

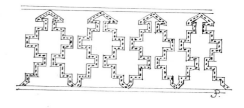

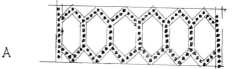

A

BEIT EL BASHA.

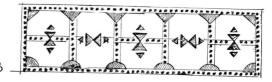

B

245. SHERIFA MIRIAM.

Other common and more Islamic motifs found were the Censer, Jar or *Misbah* (Mosque oil-lamp) and occasionally a "poplar tree" unit (Tree of Life) recalling the familiar "pomegranate" of Persia or "Paisley" motif (p. 100).

Painted designs were rare, but it is appropriate to illustrate some taken from an upper room in No. 220 which recall some of the motifs incised in *Tangil*. The lions supporting a "Tree of Life" is a touching reminder of the tenacity of this oldest of heraldic devices, traceable to Mycenæ c.1200 B.C. and even earlier (p. 102).

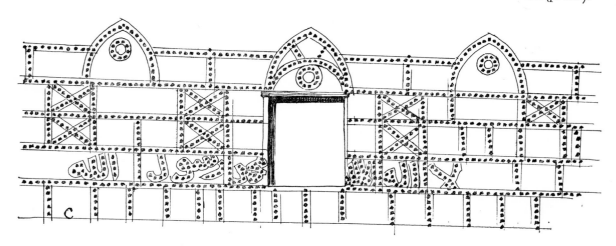

C

PLASTER
DECORATIONS
Geometric

99

KHORSHID EFF's. DIWAN. Nº 35

PLASTER
DECORATIONS
Floral

52 cm. sq.

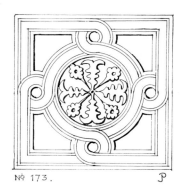

Nº 173.

100

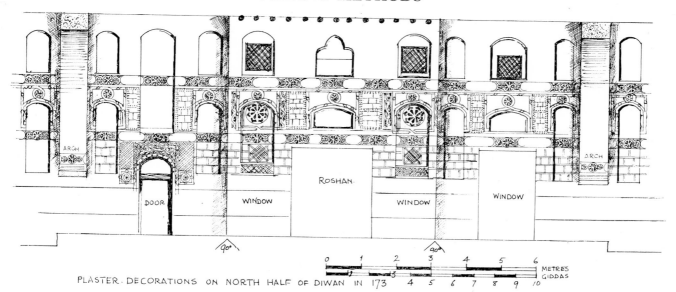

PLASTER. DECORATIONS ON NORTH HALF OF DIWAN IN 173

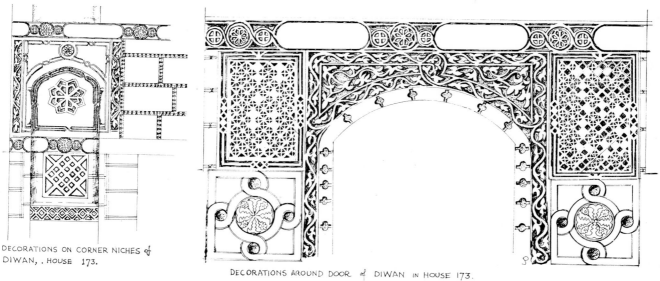

DECORATIONS ON CORNER NICHES of
DIWAN, . HOUSE 173.

DECORATIONS AROUND DOOR of DIWAN IN HOUSE 173.

**PLASTER
DECORATIONS
IN HOUSE
No. 173**

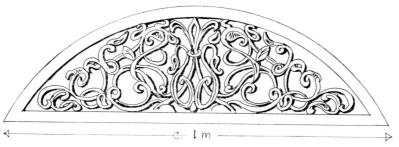

INCISED PLASTER LUNETTE. No 173.

7   DISPOSITION OF THE PAINTINGS ON THE WALLS. OF THE ROOM.

6.

5   LION & "TREE-OF-LIFE" MOTIF FRAGMENTS.

1

2

3

4

"TREE-OF-LIFE" MOTIFS FROM WALL-PAINTINGS IN HOUSE 22
Painted in RED & YELLOW OCHRE

CHAPTER ELEVEN
WOODWORK

WOODWORK is considered by some not to have been carried to a very high degree of proficiency in the Islamic world. Yet the mosques and palaces of Cairo and the houses of Jedda and Suakin contain woodwork of a very high quality despite the lack of good timber in the countries concerned. Added to this there is the long Arab tradition of boat-building. The craftsmen of Islamic countries excelled even in this material, but in Suakin it remained a mainly external, rugged and large-scale craft. The absence of wooden furniture in the domestic life of the wealthy except for *mashrabiyas*, panelled doors and small occasional tables or *kursis* meant that cabinet-work, as we know it in the West, was seldom needed. Woodwork was not therefore carried to the pitch of refinement of Sheraton or Hepplewhite except in great cities like Cairo.

The woodwork of Suakin and Jedda can be considered under three headings. First the construction of the *roshans* and windows which, in some cases, cover nearly the whole front of a building. Second, the panelled or elaborately-carved and ornamented doors such as those of Jedda and Zanzibar. Third, there are the ingenious forms of grille-work and fretted decoration, called *shish*, *shareikha*, or *sharfa* which are incorporated in the windows and *roshans* and which merit a separate study on their own.

The wood for most of this work was Java teak, called by the craftsmen, *jawi*. It is a very heavy, light-brown wood which weathers, like most woods, to a silvery grey. It was shipped in bulk by dhows from Java and the actual carving was done in Java itself.

Roshans (Mashrabiyas)

There are various kinds of *mashrabiya* design in Islamic countries and sub-divisions within each style; the style most familiar to Europeans is one made of the little, turned pieces and rods such as were usual in the *mashrabiyas* of Cairo. These were often dismantled and turned into screens and panels which travellers in the nineteenth century brought back to Europe and they could be seen in many a Victorian or Parisian drawing-room.

The typical Red Sea *mashrabiyas*, called *roshans*, however, were not of this kind. They were built up of panels and grilles of *shish* made from notched or tongued laths halved into each other at righ-angles and set within a frame. This *shish* or *shareikha* work, as it is technically called, is described separately.

The *roshans* of Suakin and Jedda varied considerably in decoration and size. The workmanship was always good but there were cheaper *roshans* with a minimum of detail and ornamental treatment. The great majority in Suakin were 2.40 m. (4 *giddas*) in width, 0.6 m. (1 *gidda*) in depth (overhanging the street), and 2.80 m. or 3 m. internal height. There are much larger ones in Jeddah. Suakin had one double-length *roshan* (House No. 155) and one double-depth (No. 86). Teak being a heavy wood, deep *roshans* are rare, but their width may extend to three or four metres. The simplest type, on the ground-floor had three bays only; the average had four in Suakin but in Jedda those with five are common. More than this number of bays is rarer.

Roshans were broadly of two types; a shaded, hooded (*burneita*[19]) type in which the top is shaded with a wide overhanging hood (*raf-raf*) which usually had a central crest, the *burneita*. The second, crowned or corniced (*jaft*) type, the head of which was crowned by a cornice but had no overhanging hood. This may be a later type since they are found better preserved and may even show European influence, being corniced like much European woodwork of the time. Again it may be due to mere economy, for the hood requires much extra work to make and repair and is the first part to drop off. A *roshan* consists of three separately-made parts:

1. A separate base or supporting bracket (*mad'af*).
2. A central portion (*jalsa*) in which one sits consisting of an open portion with its numerous shutters and traps, and a head with various kinds of ventilators.
3. Finally, at the top, there is the shade (*raf-raf*) or cornice (*jaft*) to cap the whole.

The base-bracket (*mad'af*) in which the *roshan* is set consists essentially of five or more stout timbers embedded firmly into the entire thickness of the masonry with an upward tilt of about 10°. These timbers may be hidden by decorated brackets and panels which, however, add nothing to their supporting power.

The central or main portion of the *roshan* is built-up from three independent flat frames, a front and two sides. These are assembled on the site. The base and cornice hold them in position at top and bottom. They sometimes had small, metal, angle reinforcements at the corners.

The panelling of this part of the *roshan* at the bottom is, of course, solid, but at the top, panelling is combined with *shish* ventilators to admit light and air.

In between these are the two unequal tiers of shutters. The smaller ones at the bottom fold out downwards and are supported on a bracket outside. The larger shutters fold upwards and provide extra shade as well as light and air. They are held in position by long hooks which act as stays. In the ground-floor *roshans* these shutters slide up and down in grooves like sash windows. They cannot open outwards because ground-floor windows are always barred.

The shade-hoods (*raf-raf*) on the *roshans* are wide. They descend at an angle from the top and cast a deep shadow. The addition of a fringe of wooden "stalactites" and the side-brackets (*durrah*) which support the hood increases this shade. The hood carried the crest (*burneita*) in the centre, which elegantly caps the whole.

There are also two main ways in which the base (*mad'af*) is treated. Either the *roshan* rests on a carved or decorated bracket (*kurdi*) or else straight on the exposed cantilevered beams embedded into the masonry. On the ground-floor, it may rest on stone-corbels or on a masonry plinth built up from the ground.

In Jedda, it was common to link *roshans* together vertically by joining the crown of one to the base of the other by a band of wood called a *hizam*, and as the crown is larger than the *roshan* itself, they tended to increase in size with each storey.

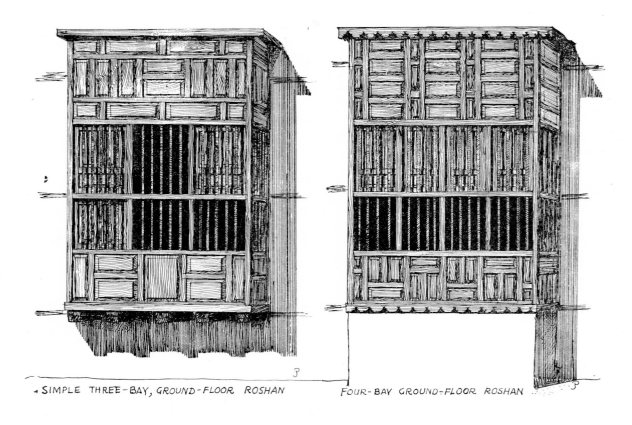

SIMPLE THREE-BAY, GROUND-FLOOR ROSHAN FOUR-BAY GROUND-FLOOR ROSHAN

Nᵒ 55   Ground Floor

Nᵒ 20   1ˢᵗ. Floor

Nᵒ 225   1ˢᵗ Floor
(Sash Shutters)

Nᵒ 25   Ground Floor

Nᵒ 132   1ˢᵗ. Floor

Nᵒ 86   Ground Floor at Rear.

Nᵒ 220   1ˢᵗ Floor

in MUKHAFAZA. 1ˢᵗ Floor.

Nᵒ 1   1ˢᵗ. Floor.

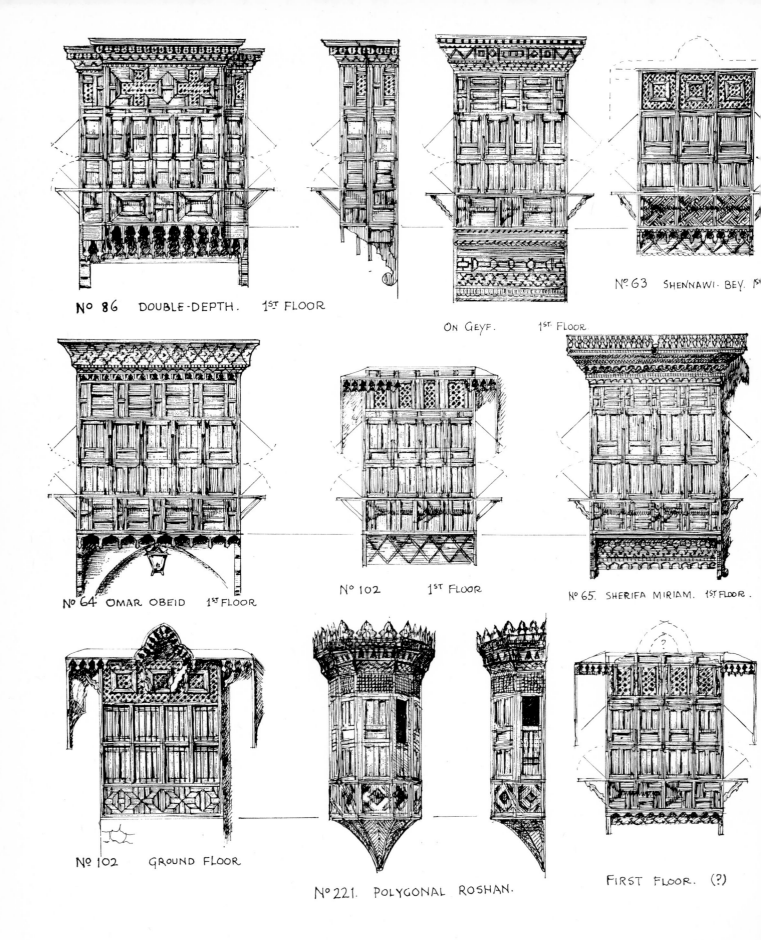

NO 86   DOUBLE-DEPTH.   1ST FLOOR

ON GEYF.   1ST FLOOR

NO 63   SHENNAWI·BEY· 1ST

NO 64   OMAR OBEID   1ST FLOOR

NO 102   1ST FLOOR

NO 65. SHERIFA MIRIAM. 1ST FLOOR.

NO 102   GROUND FLOOR

NO 221. POLYGONAL ROSHAN.

FIRST FLOOR.   (?)

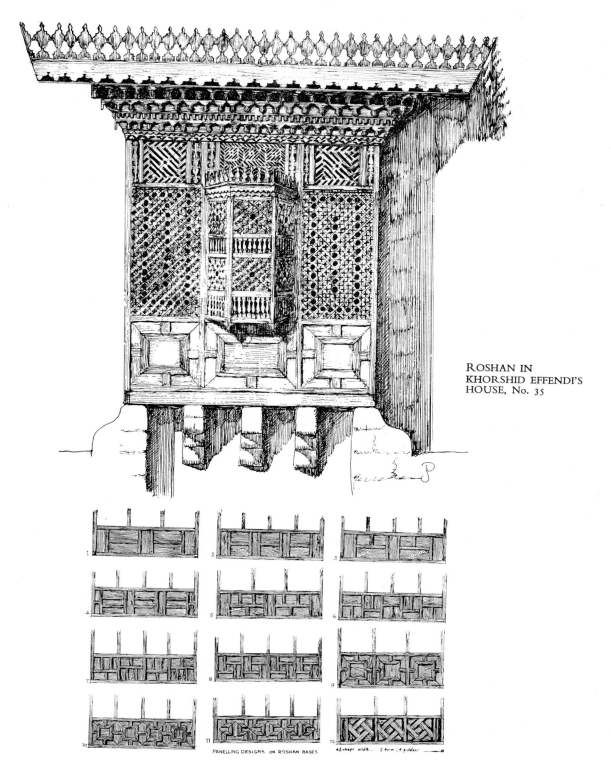

ROSHAN IN
KHORSHID EFFENDI'S
HOUSE, No. 35

1   2   3

4   5   6

7   8   9

10   11   12

PANELLING DESIGNS ON ROSHAN BASES   Average width 2.40 m (4 giddas)

107

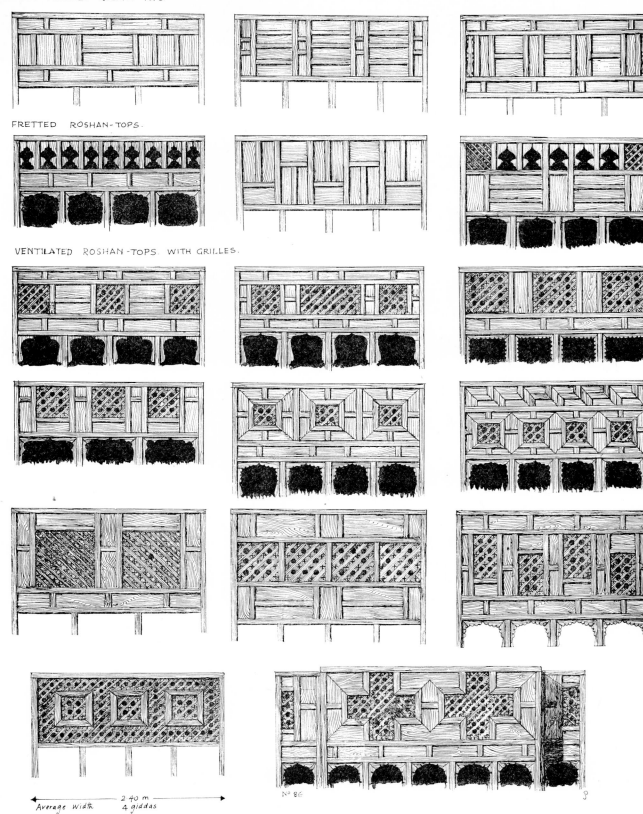

SOLID PANELLED ROSHAN-TOPS.

FRETTED ROSHAN-TOPS.

VENTILATED ROSHAN-TOPS. WITH GRILLES.

Average Width 2.40 m 4 giddas

Nº 86

GREAT ROSHANS IN HOUSE OF SHENNAWI BEY, No. 163

45 cm.

LONG HOOK FOR SUPPORTING ROSHAN - SHUTTERS

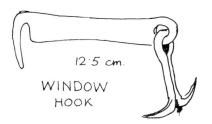

12.5 cm.

WINDOW
HOOK

The Windows (Shubbak-Shabbabik)

Windows were related in design to the *roshans* with which they formed a set. The base-panelling would usually be identical and the ventilated top-portion would have the same elements as the related *roshans*. The shades over were usually joined to the next *roshan* or windows to form a continuous band of shade across the wall of the building. The windows were of three sizes: small, medium and large. A large window was identical to the front-portion of a *roshan* and was used as a flat *roshan* to sit in if the street was too narrow to allow it to project. Above each smaller window was a ventilator, *taga*, which was let into the wall and fitted with a grille or *shish*-work; this brought the window-top up to the level of the adjoining *roshan*.

WOODWORK

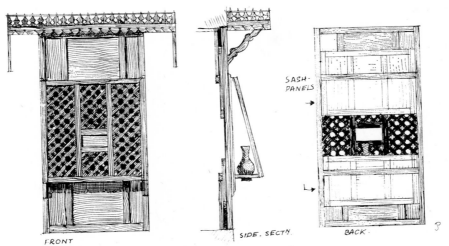

FRONT   SIDE. SECTN.   BACK.

WINDOWS IN KHORSHID EFF'S HOUSE. Nº 35

WINDOWS FROM BEIT EL BASHA. Nº 184

TYPICAL WINDOWS FROM "TURKISH" STYLE HOUSES.

WOODWORK

THE NORTH
WINDOW IN
SHENNAWI
BEY'S NEW
DIWAN
HOUSE 196

c 2·5 M

1·75 M.

LARGER TYPE

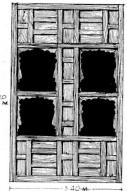

c 2·20 M

1·40 M.

INTERMEDIATE SIZE

III

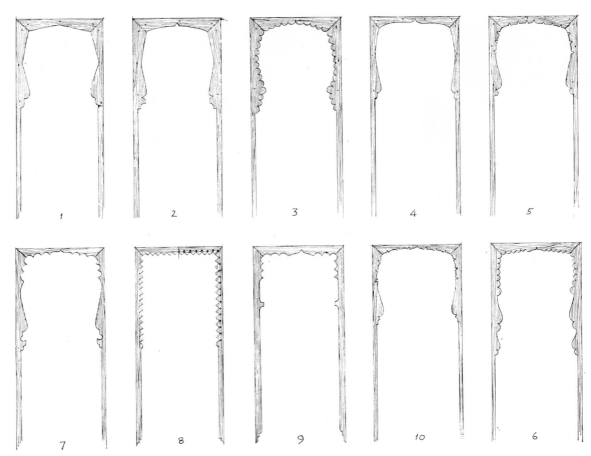

FRAMES TO DOOR -(AND WINDOW) -APERTURES.

Suakin had only a few examples of large woodwork panelling, notably the window over the entrance-gate of the Wakala, the window to the *diwan* in Shennawi Bey's new house (No. 196) and two *salas* in House No. 86. These last were flat areas of window rather larger than usual. In Jedda, two sides of a whole upper room might be built of panelled woodwork with grilles, traps and elaborately worked cornices.

Fretted Frames ('Agd) for Doors and Windows

Most rectangular openings, whether on windows, *roshans*, *tagas* or doors, were framed with fretted arches or *'agd*. There were many designs. They were applied to the insides of windows, *roshans* and door-openings.

External Doors

The street-doors of Suakin were mostly made of plain panelling with little decoration. One door alone, that of Khorshid Effendi, had elaborately carved panels but raised ovals and diamond panels were to be found.

Front doors, like the *roshans*, were solidly built of Java teak, from 75 mm. to 100 mm. thick. They were always double and pivoted about their outer edge which was extended to form lugs let into the stone threshold at the bottom, and wooden lintel at the top. This pivoting-edge was protected by a rebate in the masonry. The join of the two leaves was also protected by a large, carved fillet called the *anf* which was always decorated even in the simplest doors. This important part of the door was sometimes very large.

WOODWORK

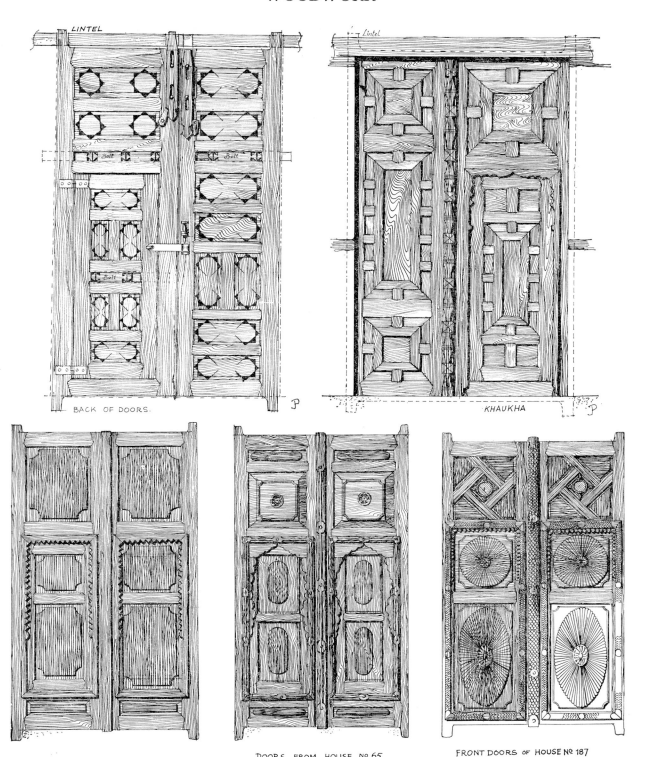

LINTEL

Bolt   Bolt

Bolt

BACK OF DOORS.

Lintel

KHAUKHA

DOORS FROM HOUSE № 65

FRONT DOORS OF HOUSE № 187

113

WOODWORK

FRONT DOORS OF HOUSE Nº 78.

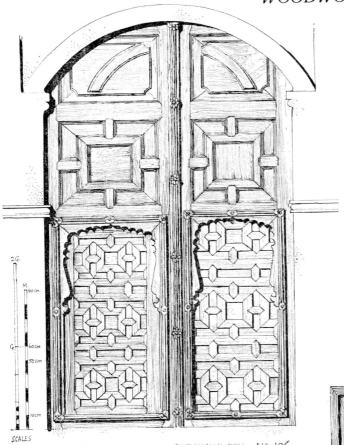

ENTRANCE DOORS TO DIWAN OF SHENNAWI BEY. Nº 196.

DOOR INTO YARD of SAYED EL SAFI'S HOUSE Nº 221.

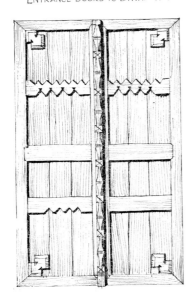

SIMPLE DOOR IN YARD of BEIT EL BASHA. 184.

114

DOOR OF KHORSHID EFFENDI'S EXTENSION. 19TH Cent.

DOOR·JAMB
(MUHAFAZA)

WOODWORK

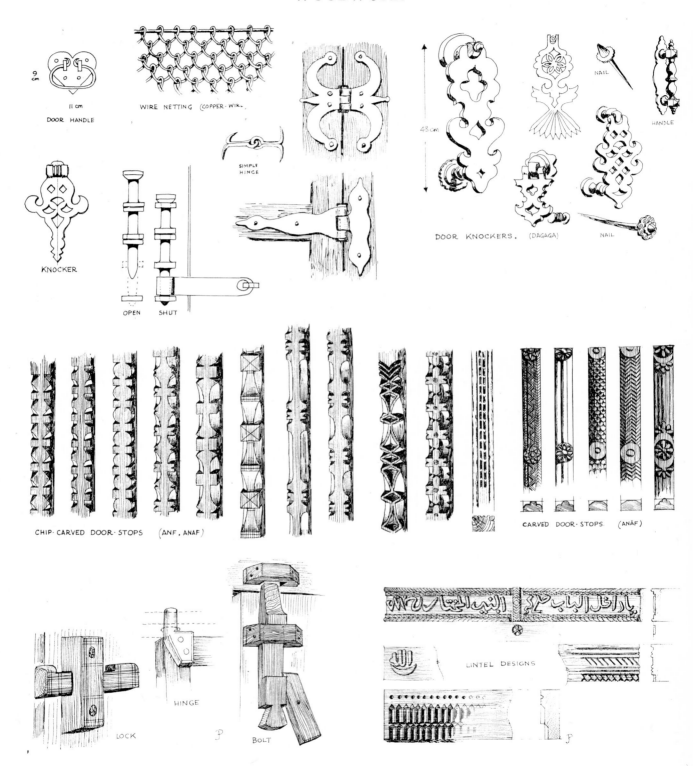

DOOR HANDLE

11 cm

9 cm

WIRE NETTING (COPPER-WIRE)

SIMPLE HINGE

43 cm

DOOR KNOCKERS. (DAGAGA)

NAIL

HANDLE

NAIL

KNOCKER

KNOCKER

OPEN   SHUT

CHIP·CARVED DOOR·STOPS   (ANF, ANAF)

CARVED DOOR·STOPS   (ANĀF)

LOCK

HINGE

BOLT

LINTEL DESIGNS

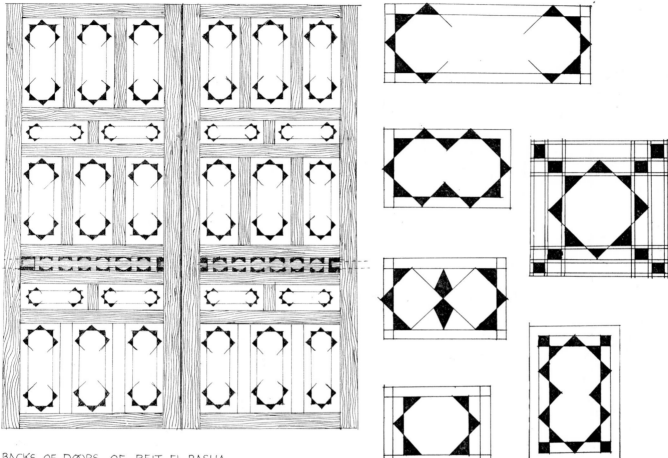

BACKS OF DOORS OF BEIT EL BASHA.

The right-hand leaf of most house doors had a smaller door let into it called a *khaukha*. It was through this that access to the house was normally obtained. The main portion was only opened to admit large loads. This little door was surrounded by its own carved, arch-shaped fillet (*'agd*) and a twin was placed round the corresponding part of the other leaf. All openings like doors and windows were surrounded by such *'agds*. They served to cover the chinks and provided a decorative frame when the door was open.

The method of bolting and barring these doors was ingenious. The back often had built-in sliding wooden bolts which protruded into the stone jambs as well as into the other leaf of the door. Metal bolts, studs (*musmar kawkab*) and knockers (*dagaga*) were also used.

All doors were two-leaved, even store and cupboard-doors. A two-leaved door takes up less room than a single one. They opened into the thickness of the wall which they seldom exceeded in width, and so they took up no space at all within the room itself.

Internal and Cupboard Doors

These were of lighter construction and sometimes carved, painted or decorated with a simple etched pattern. The built-in shelves sometimes had doors to make them into cupboards.

Internal doorways were usually surmounted by large grilled apertures reaching up to the ceiling to allow the air to circulate throughout the house.

INTERIOR CARVED CUPBOARD DOORS.

INTERIOR CARVED DOORS IN BEIT EL BASHA   № 184

INTERNAL CUPBOARD DOORS.

Panelling (Khashwa)

The panelling deserves a separate mention, though it is but a part of a *roshan*, window or door, for it contains a variety of patterns and styles on its own. The craft is seen at its most elaborate in Cairo where the patterns are ingenious and complicated. In Jedda there are also many fine examples.

The work is of two main kinds: plain rectangular, or complex geometric designs usually diagonally placed. It is also either flush or raised. The latter patterns are usually based on the hexagon (*museddis* or *'agli*), and octagon (*mutamin*). There are two further patterns called *Abu taranga* and *maghrabiya* (the latter presumably from the west of Islam, the *Maghreb*). Some of the commoner patterns are illustrated here. There were no two *roshans* alike in Suakin but the few different component units that I could trace could be combined indefinitely without repetition.

Panelling was applied to the other woodwork pieces such as doors, wooden archways or room-dividers, and mosque pulpits (*minbars*).

WOODWORK

MUTAMIN (OCTAGONAL) DESIGN   منامن

MAGHRABIYA DESIGN (Western Style) (FLUSH PANELLING)   مغربية

MA'AGLI TARNAJ DESIGN   FLUSH PANELLING.   معقلي ترنج

MUSEDDIS (HEXAGONAL) DESIGN (RAISED PANELLING) مسدّس

120

WOODEN DIVIDING ARCH IN GT DIWAN OF SHENNAWI BEY'S NEW HOUSE N° 196.

Internal Wooden Archways

Large *diwans* were divided into two sections by an archway. Those on the ground-floor were built of masonry, but on the upper-floors they were made of wood. Their function was primarily to support the ceiling timbers and often the wall of the room above. They also marked off the seated portion or *iwan* of the room from the entrance portion. These archways were carved and ornamented and were made in different ways. Two types are shown here. A third, Egyptian (*Kharati*) type in the Muhafaza is shown on p. 122, it is made of small turned pieces and is common in Cairo. It is the only example of this work in Suakin.

WOODEN ARCHWAY AT HARÎM MAJLIS OF HOUSE N° 1.

WOODWORK

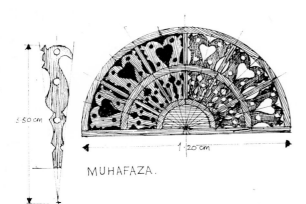

MUHAFAZA.

DOOR-LIGHT & VENTILATOR   Nº 103
MITCHELL COTTS.

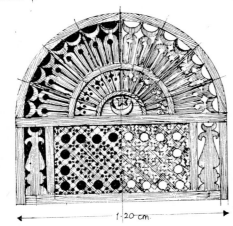

Nº 22 MOH. BEY AHMED. (FIRST FLOOR)

FRETTED WOODEN LUNETTES.   (EGYPTIAN STYLE)

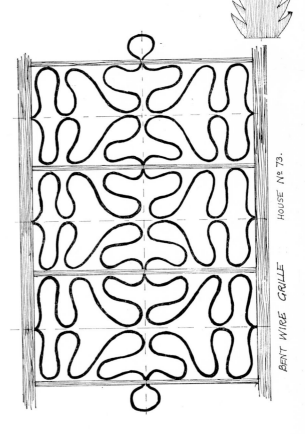

BENT WIRE GRILLE   HOUSE Nº 73.

WROUGHT-IRON GRILLE *from*
THE LAWCOURTS.

Lattice-work grilles (Shish or Shareikha)

In hot climates where shade, combined with the circulation of cool air is desirable, lattice-work best serves this double purpose. It also serves as a screen from strangers. From the inside, it forms a net-like veil over the view outside and throws shadow-patterns on the floor and objects within the room. It is more suitable than glass which becomes unpleasantly hot in the tropics acting like a hot-plate in the wall. *Shish* is a functional lattice which has been carried to a considerable degree of refinement in the East, especially in Cairo, in the "turned" style (*kharati*) already described. In Jedda and Suakin, a criss-cross, notched and slatted type was usual. It was mainly confined to small rectangular insets in a larger pattern of panels but was sometimes large enough to cover a whole window or *roshan*-top (p. 126).

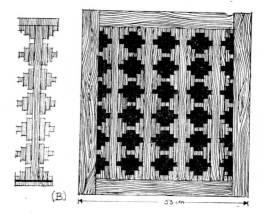

(B.) 53 cm

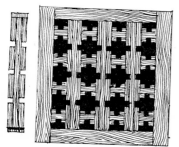

GRILLES WITH CRISS-CROSS LATHS. (A)

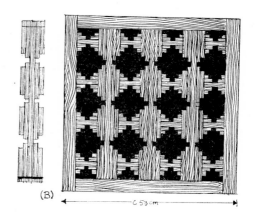

(B) C 53 cm

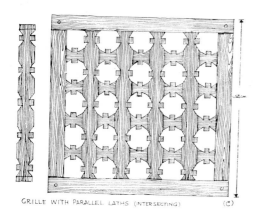

GRILLE WITH PARALLEL LATHS (INTERSECTING) (C)

GRILLES WITH PARALLEL LATHS. (A)

Large Protective Grilles

There was a large, simple form of grille used mainly on the ground-floor at the back of a building to prevent entrance through low-placed windows such as are to be found in mosques or outbuildings and to illuminate the stairways. It consisted of vertical and horizontal wooden bars blocking an opening, but the manner in which the bars were notched and spaced produced a simple pattern and lifted them above the purely functional.

LARGE GRILLE FOR MOSQUES.

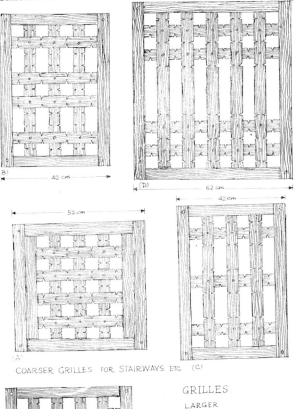

(B) 42 cm

(D) 62 cm

52 cm

42 cm

COARSER GRILLES FOR STAIRWAYS ETC. (C)

GRILLES
LARGER

53 cm (B)
LARGER MORTICE & TENON TYPE (Parallel)

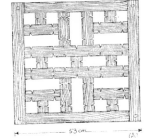

53 cm (A)

Tenoned Grilles

There was a kind of *shish* which was tenoned together (*malaj*). It was rarer than the criss-cross kind and appeared on older buildings. It was similar to Chinese lattice-work and consisted of a series of small wooden laths of rectangular section tenoned into each other at right-angles, the narrow edge towards the front. The pieces never crossed each other; they met in "T" or "H" joints. There were different sizes, but the small size was rare. One example was to be found on the *roshan* of the house of Khorshid Effendi, (36) another on a *roshan* in the house of Shennawi Bey (163). The laths of the larger variety were laid parallel to the sides of the frame.

124

WOODWORK

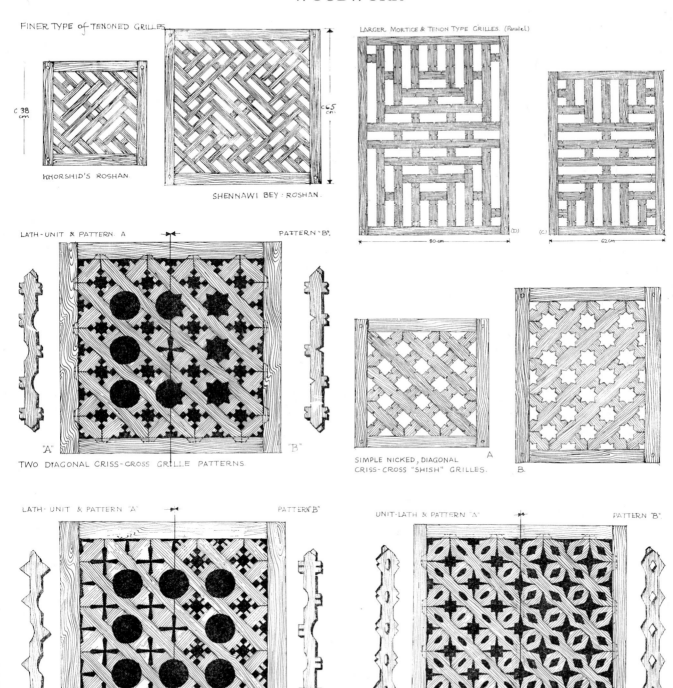

FINER TYPE of TENONED GRILLES.

c 38 cm

KHORSHID'S ROSHAN.

c 65 cm

SHENNAWI BEY : ROSHAN.

LARGER MORTICE & TENON TYPE GRILLES. (Parallel)

80 cm (D)

62 cm (C)

LATH-UNIT & PATTERN "A"

PATTERN "B".

"A"   "B"

TWO DIAGONAL CRISS-CROSS GRILLE PATTERNS.

SIMPLE NICKED, DIAGONAL
CRISS-CROSS "SHISH" GRILLES.

A

B.

LATH-UNIT & PATTERN "A"

PATTERN "B"

"A"   "B"

TWO CRISS-CROSS GRILLE PATTERNS.

UNIT-LATH & PATTERN "A"

PATTERN "B".

A   B.

TWO PERFORATED, DIAGONAL, CRISS-CROSS "SHISH" GRILLE.

VENTILATED TOP OF SALA FROM HOUSE 86, NOW IN MUHAFAZA.

HEAD OF ROSHAN OF HOUSE N° 273.

WOODWORK

from Beit el Basha.

BRACKET-SHELVES IN MAJLIS 220.

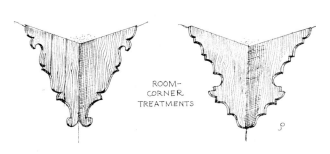

ROOM-
CORNER
TREATMENTS

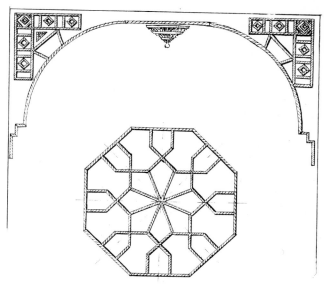

TACKED LATH DECORATIONS ON ARCH AND
CIELING OF ROSHAN IN HOUSE 220.

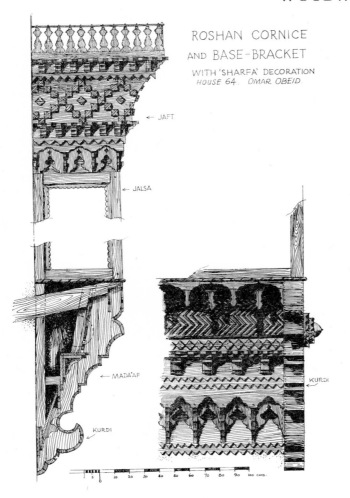

ROSHAN CORNICE
AND BASE-BRACKET

WITH 'SHARFA' DECORATION
HOUSE 64. OMAR OBEID.

← JAFT

← JALSA

← MADA'AF

KURDI →

KURDI

ROSHAN CORNICES AND BRACKETS

ROSHAN CORNICE
AND BASE-BRACKET
WITH 'SHARFA' DECORATION.

DRILLED DECORATION. A.

DRILLED
DECORATION. B.

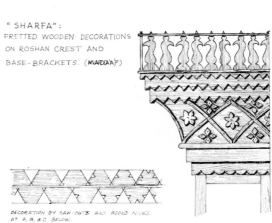

"SHARFA":
FRETTED WOODEN DECORATIONS
ON ROSHAN CREST AND
BASE-BRACKETS. (MADA'AF)

DECORATION BY SAW-CUTS AND ADDED NICKS
AT A, B, & C BELOW.

Fretted and Tacked Decorations (Sharfa)

Later *roshans*, windows, doors and cupboards were sometimes finished off with designs composed of fret-worked pieces tacked onto them. Many wooden surfaces were treated in this way in the later Arab buildings. Finicky as the work sometimes seems, the patterns were usually made from a simple, basic unit easily cut from a length of wood. Several thicknesses were clamped together and cut out at once. The pieces were then reversed and placed edge to edge. The portions removed also made negative symmetrical patterns and were used elsewhere. Notching the edges and drilling of holes were also used for decorative effect.

When this ornament, which was reserved for the *tagas*, *roshans* and doorways, was seen in relation to the facade as a whole with its large areas of plain, white wall, it made a wholesome contrast. This contrast of large plain areas with small highly-decorated ones is characteristic of Islamic Architecture.

Sharfa work was of various sorts:

(a) The kind already described on p. 112 as *'aqds* which framed symmetrical openings.

(b) A kind which was seen in silhouette standing out against the sky or house-wall — in *roshan-*crests or hanging in stalactites on bases. These were often the parts cut out of the first kind. Some of these were cut into stylized bird silhouettes.

(c) A flat kind called *bandaroon* which was tacked onto a plain, unadorned background, a cornice, *hizam* or other portion of woodwork, to make surface-designs.

(d) It was also used to make centralising features for a panel or ceiling.

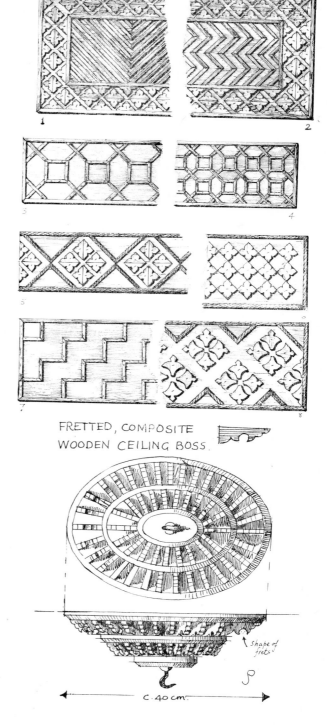

TACKED & FRETTED WOODEN DECORATIONS ON ROSHAN-BASES.

FRETTED, COMPOSITE WOODEN CEILING BOSS.

c. 40 cm.

shape of frets

Carved Wooden Ornaments: Ceiling-Bosses

Ornaments were also built-up from a number of fretted pieces arranged radially or superimposed upon each other concentrically.

Pendants for Lanterns were turned, or carved with an adze, like table-legs, and embedded in the centre of an arch of masonry. They had a hook at the end from which the lantern was suspended.

Metalwork (p. 116)

Metalwork was not extensive in Suakin. Wrought-iron was introduced in the Egyptian period. A few metal objects in brass and bronze are worth noting:

1. Hooks for *roshans* beaten out of a flat piece of soft iron. They had a characteristic flattened ratchet to hold the flap open (p. 109).
2. Hinges for small doors in recessed shelves consisted simply of two circular eyes made like split-pins driven through the wood and bent over.
3. Wire-netting from soft brass wire. A bent-wire decoration for a grille. Over a doorway.
4. Ornamental studs (*musmar kawkab*) for doors; there were many designs.
5. Door-knockers (*dagaga*). These were of many designs in Jedda; some were very heavy and elaborately cut. There were few in Suakin.
6. Wrought-iron grilles and lunettes above doors and windows in Egyptian-style houses (p. 122).
7. Metal Lanterns (p. 131).

Furniture

I found a few abandoned objects of furniture in store-rooms which are worth recording:

1. A circular three-footed column table with horse-shaped feet. This is now in the *Muhafaza*.
2. A child's cart, (but without its wheels).
3. A wheeled-stand to teach a baby to walk.
4. A tea-chest cheaply converted into a decorated travelling-trunk.
5. A seat or child's cot with protective turned rail.

Outside furniture. Lying propped against the walls of Beit Siam were two large pieces of woodwork, rather like the top of an old capstan. It was not until a later visit that I saw them being used for their true purpose, a child's vertical merry-go-round, called a *murjaiha*. They were still there under a pile of rubble on the author's last visit to Suakin in 1974 (p. 16).

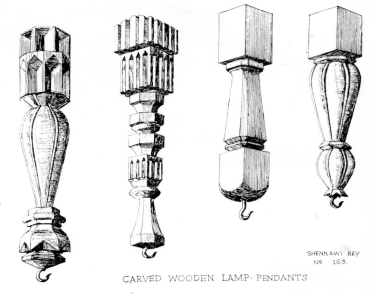

SHENNAWI BEY
Nº 163.

CARVED WOODEN LAMP-PENDANTS

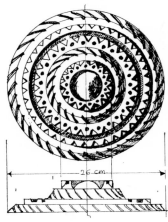

CIRCULAR DOOR-BOSS.

FRETTED WOOD FILLET.

Outside one of the mosques lay a derelict bier-stretcher (*nagala*). It had wire hoops for supporting a protective cloth covering and was used for "important" burials.

WOODWORK

WOODEN BOSS ON MAIN DOOR OF WAKKALA.

FRETTED RAIN-
SPOUT TERMINAL

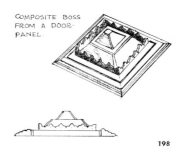

COMPOSITE BOSS
FROM A DOOR-
PANEL.

198

METAL LANTERNS

chimney on external street-lamp.

1

2

3

4 covered in material.

5

6

7 ZEI

8 CLOTH COVERED.

9 P.

131

POSTSCRIPT

The remarkable thing about Suakin was its compact unity, a quality easily appreciable by reason of its size and island situation. This quality accounts for the fascination certain places have. It is a quality hard to find in such completeness to-day. In Western Europe such places attract tourists who find in them a rare architectural experience. Carcassonne (rebuilt in the nineteenth century) and many little hill-towns in Southern France, such as Cagnes and S. Paul de Vence, and in Italy, S. Gimigniano, S. Remo, and the Greek-Islands all have it and are well-known and admired.

But the situation of Suakin on its flat circular island showed off its unity to perfection, and on closer inspection this quality could be traced down to the repeated motifs in decoration, whether they were in wood, plaster, or carved in stone, engraved on metalwork or painted on pottery, embroidered on curtains or garments, or contrived in the ornaments worn by the women. All spoke with one tongue.

This unity betokens deep social agreement and a corporate belief which accompanies the all-pervading metaphysical system and religion of Islam.

NOTES

[1] *The Twentieth Century Decline of Suakin* by D. Roden. 1970. Published by the Sudan Research Unit of the University of Khartoum.

[2] SSD Towns 7951/2. 1916. Drawn by C. Bryce.

[3] *Kush* The Archaeological Periodical published by the Antiquities Service in the Sudan.

[4] This brief historical summary is taken from a fuller account by Dr Bloss in *Sudan Notes and Records*, Vol. XIV (1936) part II, and Vol. XX (1937) part II, which also gives references.
1A. E. Robinson *Arab Dynasty of Darfur. Journal of African Soc.* October.

[5] Wylde, 83-87 *in the Sudan* Vol. II, p. 277.

[6] From the Arabic *"darwish"* as the followers of Mahdi came to be known in Egypt and the West. In the Sudan they were (and still are) known as the *Ansar* — or "supporters".

[7] A tall four-storey building built around an inner well-like courtyard and demolished before this survey was finished.

[8] For a recent study of this period see D. Roden, *The Twentieth Century Decline of Suakin* University of Khartoum, 1970.

[9] Dried-out gourd core; *lif* in the Sudan.

[10] The word *mashrabiya* is derived from the Arabic *sharaba*, to drink, for, in Egypt and other moslem lands, these bay-windows usually contain porous earthenware jars called *gullas* for drinking-water which is kept cool by evaporation. Another theory is that it is a corruption of *mashrafiya*, from *sharafa*, to peer or peep, for the occupants could gaze into the street below without being seen themselves. In the Red Sea however, they are called a *roshan* (plural *rawashin*), the origin of which is Persian and means "light". The window is considered, as in Europe, as a source of light as well as of air. The presence of a Persian word in Jedda and Suakin is due to the fact that the makers of these *roshans* were from Bokhara and had settled in Jeddah for generations. cf. Roden op. cit.

[11] "Hubble-bubble" smoking pipe, which can be shared by many people each one plugging-in his own personal mouthpiece to the end of a long flexible tube; it is called a *shish* in the Sudan.

[12] Sudan Notes and Records, 1931.

[13] cf. Bloss, "The Story of Suakin", Sudan Notes and Records Vol. XX Part III 1937 p. 279, 5, vi.

[14] See E. Pauty *Palais et Maisons de l'époque Musulmane au Caire* Published by l'Institut Français d'Archéologie Orientale au Caire. Vol. 62 1932.

[15] *Iwan* or *liwan* is the term used for this raised part of a room or divan in Cairo houses. See E. Pauty op. cit.

[16] cf. Bloss, op. cit.

[17] The *gidda* measured in Jedda by the author was approximately 60 cm. and his drawings and their accompanying comparative scales are based on this fact. He learnt only subsequently that the *dhira'a* is 58 cm. If the measures are the same in fact, his drawings will contain a 4% error. He acknowledges this now irremediable discrepancy with regret.

[18] D. H. Matthews "The Red Sea Style" *Kush*, Vol. 1, 1954, for the similarity of this technique with building-methods in Ethiopia and Byzantium, especially what he calls 'monkey' joints which are to be seen in stylized form on the stone obelisks of Axum and elsewhere in Ethiopia.

[19] The word *"burneita"* is also applied in the Sudan to European-type brimmed hats and motorcar "bonnets" (from which the word itself may be derived). *Raf-raf* was also applied to motorcar mudguards and running-boards.